7 Steps to Purpose

Tom and Pam Wolf

Identity and Destiny – 7 Steps to a Purpose-Filled Life
by Tom and Pam Wolf

Printed in the United States of America

ISBN 9781613790328

www.xulonpress.com

Acknowledgments

Without the loving encouragement of family and friends, and the expertise of professionals who have been part of this project, the **7 Steps** would still be a dream in our hearts rather than a workbook in print. It is with the utmost gratitude that we offer our thanks!

Writer and Editor: Vickie Parsons
Editor and Reviewer: Sean Fowlds
Proofreader: Linda Miller
Graphics and Cover Design: Ty Schafrath
Layout Specialist: Kara Spence
Original Music: Jacob Hamby

Publisher: Xulon Press

Draft Critiques: John Stone, Robert Leatherwood, Debbie Ferguson, Jan Karamitsanis, Amanda and Jonah Mayhall, Ted Wolf, Missy Steadman and Daniel Bernard

Website Design Team: Juan Espinosa, Bob Bardel and Vision 1 Media

We offer special thanks to our pastor, Matthew Hartsfield – Van Dyke Church – for his blessing and support. Through his Godly wisdom, teaching and example, we continue to grow in Christ under his leadership.

Most of all we thank the Lord for the opportunity to serve others and grow closer to Him in faith as He shepherds us every step of the way.

About the Authors

Statistics show that **only 3% of people ever find their true life's purpose**. Most never take the time or make the effort. Those who do often become frustrated as they struggle to figure out how to actually find it.

That's why husband and wife team, Tom and Pam Wolf, are so passionate about the process of purpose discovery. They have created and written the **7 Steps to Purpose** to provide a step-by-step guide to help you FIND, KNOW, and LIVE your God-given purpose. This workbook is not just theory—it is a practical process providing tangible results that will transform your life.

Before embarking on their personal search for purpose—which ultimately resulted in the **7 Steps**—Tom and Pam had decades of experience as successful entrepreneurs. They each earned advanced business degrees and enjoyed leading and developing both the people and the organizations they built over their 30 years in business. (For full details on their background and careers, please visit www.IdentityandDestiny.com.)

Most importantly, you need to know that Tom and Pam are now taking their experience and applying it to the purpose God has revealed for their lives. Through *Identity and Destiny*, they are passionately focused on helping others discover and unleash the power of purpose.

Tom and Pam are part of the 3% who clearly know their purpose and they want you to join them. Their purpose in life is to help you find yours!

They are eager to faithfully share the **7 Steps to Purpose** with all who are ready to embark on this exciting journey—the journey of discovering your God-given purpose. Are you ready?

Here's what the authors want you to know:

- God loves you and has a specific plan for your life.
- You are one-of-a-kind and uniquely designed to fulfill your purpose.
- You will never be truly satisfied until you find that purpose.
- The plans and purpose God has for your life matter—both here and in eternity.
- God wants to touch your life and use you in ways you can only imagine.

Begin your journey of discovery today.

7 Steps in 8 Weeks: You do the steps—God does the rest!

Introduction

Everyone, at one point or another, stops what they're doing and wonders: "What on earth am I doing here?"

The **7 Steps to Purpose** is written to answer the question "Who am I?" so that the response to "Why am I here?" takes advantage of everything God has given you: the good, the bad, the blessings, and the struggles. They are all part of God's magnificent plan for you and you alone.

Completing the **7 Steps** program will:

- Help you discover your God-given strengths, gifts, and passion.
- Help you take the events of your past and either smooth a path through them or put them to good use.
- Provide deep self-awareness and acceptance.
- Open your heart and mind to a more intimate relationship with the Lord.
- Give you a purpose-centered plumb line for choices and decisions.
- Positively impact every aspect of your life: career, family, finances, and relationships.
- Help you FIND your God-given purpose and LIVE a life you truly love!

SOUND GOOD? HERE'S HOW IT ALL STARTED:

Our careers—in fact, our entire lives—have been focused on helping people develop their full potential. Whether it was as business owners, executive coaches, or parents, our emphasis has always been helping people recognize and focus their strengths in ways that result in deeper personal satisfaction and greater success. We have now taken those decades of experience and applied them to helping others learn how the Lord can reveal His plans—if they will take time to genuinely seek Him for the answers.

HERE'S HOW IT WORKS

We've refined the process of searching for purpose into a series of seven steps that are detailed in this workbook. (For a quick overview of the steps, take a look at the Table of Contents that follows.) The process is designed for both individual and small group study. Either way, in just seven steps over the next eight weeks, you can clearly define the Lord's purpose for your life.

I know the plans I have for you, declares the Lord. Plans to prosper you and not to harm you; plans to give you hope and a future. Jeremiah 29:11

With the **7 Steps to Purpose**, you now have a way to discover that plan!

IS THIS PROGRAM RIGHT FOR ME?

- First, you must believe there is a God.
- Next, you must assume that the Bible is a credible source of wisdom and guidance.
- You believe that you were created by God and therefore have a God-given purpose that is unique and individually given. As it says in Jeremiah 1:5:

  Before I formed you in the womb, I knew you. Before you were born, I set you apart.
- You accept that all of the events in your life (good and bad, great and small) can be used by the Lord to build the abilities, attitudes, skills, and character needed to execute on your purpose.
- Finally, you have a genuine desire to FIND, KNOW, and LIVE your God-given purpose.

If you can say "yes" to these five assumptions, the **7 Steps to Purpose** is the right program for you!

KEYS FOR SUCCESS

The following are important keys for success as you begin the program:

- Stay open-minded, receptive, and possibility-oriented. Be willing to learn and explore, to be honest and transparent. Be open to the Lord and trust the process.
- Control the skeptical, judgmental, and critical chatter in your mind so it doesn't dominate, interrupt or keep you from getting all you can from the process.
- Avoid turning off your brain by thinking you already know what's being taught. Be willing to learn, grow and go deeper.
- Think "outside the box" — and get ready for an eight week journey that will lead you down profoundly revealing roads of personal discovery.

KNOW THIS: Nothing of value comes in life without time and effort. And although the **7 Steps** program will require both, we can assure you it's an amazing process that will change your life for the better…forever!
You do the steps—God does the rest!

Enjoy your journey!

Tom and Pam

Contents

Phase I: *The Intellectual Phase Weeks 1-4*

WELCOME 11
Purpose Scorecard
7 Steps to Purpose
3 Elements of Purpose
Your Purpose Mosaic

STEP 1: HOW ARE YOU WIRED? 41
Personality Style Analysis
Resilience Quotient

STEP 2: WHAT MAKES YOU TICK? 81
Top 5 Core Values
Dominant Spiritual Gift

STEP 3: WHAT'S YOUR PASSION? 119
Passion Pursuit
Needs Beneath The Passion

Phase II: *The Bridge Week 5*

STEP 4: WHAT'S STOPPING YOU? 145
Roadblocks to Purpose
Fears, Blocks and Limiting Beliefs
Smoothing a Path to Purpose

Phase III: *The Spiritual Phase Weeks 6-8*

STEP 5: CAN YOU HEAR GOD SPEAKING? 181
Prayer of Commitment
Dreams
Purposeful Prayer
Meditation

STEP 6: CAN YOU BE STILL AND LISTEN? 217
Guided Listening Prayer
Dialogue Journaling

STEP 7: WHO AM I? AND WHY AM I HERE? 249
Assemble the Mosaic
Crystallize Your Purpose Statements
Validation and Next Steps
The Challenge

7 Steps in 8 Weeks: You do the steps—God does the rest!

WEEK ONE

Welcome

PURPOSE SCORECARD

7 STEPS TO PURPOSE

3 ELEMENTS OF PURPOSE

YOUR PURPOSE MOSAIC

Day 1 | *Welcome*

Welcome to the **7 Steps to Purpose**, a step-by-step guide to discovering the unique and individual purpose God has planned for your life!

Through the pages of this workbook and the *Identity and Destiny* process, you are embarking on the journey of a lifetime. It is a journey of personal discovery that will answer the questions: Who am I? and Why am I here?

God tells us clearly: ***I know the plans I have for you. Jeremiah 29:11***

Yet, this universal question remains: What does God have planned for ME?

In the weeks ahead, you will be able to answer that question with power and certainty. You will discover your God-given purpose and gain the clarity and freedom to live a life you truly love.

Sound good? Let's get started!

We will be your guides on this exciting journey, so let us introduce ourselves. We are Tom and Pam Wolf. We are living our God-given purpose through the *Identity and Destiny* program. We are passionate about our work, and we are living lives we truly love. To learn more about us, visit our website at www.IdentityandDestiny.com.

The **7 Steps** program was originally created to be delivered by trained coaches and counselors on an individual and small-group basis. With careful attention to detail, we have translated the program into this workbook. While the workbook has been designed to work in an individual or small group format, we've written it as though we are talking to you one-on-one. We want the experience to be highly individual and uniquely meaningful. Just as God's plan for your life is personal—so is the journey!

To maintain the personal nature of the program, we encourage you to visit the resource section on our website specifically dedicated to workbook participants. Go to www.IdentityandDestiny.com, and click on the Resources tab. There you will find additional information and referrals for digging deeper into each of the areas we address in this program. We encourage you to sign up on the site, make comments on our blog, email us your questions, and become an active part of our online community. Above all, whether you are doing this study on your own or with a small group of friends, we want you to have all the resources you need to discover your God-given purpose.

ROAD MAP FOR THE JOURNEY

In this world of smart phones, Internet access, and GPS guidance, it is increasingly uncomfortable to go anywhere without a map and detailed directions in hand. With that in mind, let us lay out your road map:

7 Steps in 8 Weeks

- **Welcome** (Week 1)
- **Steps 1 - 3:** The intellectual phase of the process (Weeks 2 – 4)
- **Step 4:** The bridge (Week 5)
- **Steps 5 - 7:** Asking God for His plan (Weeks 6 – 8)

Each of the eight weeks is divided into five daily lessons. Some days may take a little longer than others, but we've done this to allow full completion of the topic being covered. At the end of each day there will be a brief section called **"Wrapping It Up."**

In addition, there will be a **"Review"** at the end of each week. Both are designed to help you capture the essence of what you are learning and summarize it for future reference.

The end goal or destination is going to be the creation of your own personal Identity and Destiny statements. We are laying out this road map because we are going to cover a lot of ground before we get there. If you don't take time to capture your insights, it will be nearly impossible to recall everything in the later stages of the program. We will remind you with questions to prompt your thinking—but for now, we just want you to understand why we're asking you to do these daily and weekly reviews.

You will also see sections throughout the program called **"Dive Deeper."** This is a place where we will offer additional resources. If you would like to go deeper and learn more, we'll direct you to books, websites and sources with more information.

On a number of occasions throughout the **7 Step** program, we will direct you to the Resource section of the Identity and Destiny website. This is where you will find a list of all the Dive Deeper resources, as well as, additional components required to complete certain steps in the process.

Before You Go Any Further
Take time now and go to www.IdentityandDestiny.com. Click on the Resources tab at the top of the home page and become familiar with how to access all the valuable tools in the Resources area of our site.

You can also access this area of our website with this direct link:
http//:www.identityanddestiny.com/7-steps-resources.php

Finally, let us offer a couple TRAVELING TIPS for the journey:

- Take each step as it comes.
- Don't try to read too much into any one step or exercise.
- Don't worry about right or wrong.
- Collect the information and seek God for His insight.
- Immerse yourself fully in each exercise and, most of all, enjoy yourself!

If you will do your part—by faithfully working the steps—we're certain you will see why we say:

You do the steps—God does the rest!

WHO ARE YOU?

Whenever we have the opportunity to speak about the **7 Steps to Purpose**, we begin by asking participants to answer the question: Who are you?

Take a few moments and give a concise, one-sentence answer to each of the following questions:

97 percent of people never find their true purpose in life

Who are you?

What is your purpose in life?

If you're like most people, your answers describe what you do: I'm an entrepreneur, I work in sales, I'm a teacher, a volunteer, a spouse, a parent, a caregiver, a facilitator, a golfer, a gardener, or a chess player. The list could go on and on, depending upon your job, hobbies, interests, or current role in life.

All those answers may be perfectly valid, but remember, we asked, "Who *are* you?" not "What do you *do*?"

In today's culture, personal identity is most often defined by what we do. Beyond our jobs or roles in life, the majority of us don't have any idea who we are. This is especially true in the case of career professionals. They identify themselves solely as CEO, top sales rep, district manager, or some other title gained along the way. But that is not the only place you see this happen. Look at the "empty nester syndrome" when children leave home. Some parents—particularly mothers—experience a lack of identity beyond this role that leaves them lost and occasionally even clinically depressed.

This cultural norm of your job being your only identity can be a dangerous proposition. When it ends—and it will—you have no identity. That is why many of us have such a deep longing for purpose. Somewhere in our souls, we know there is more to life than our jobs, roles, and careers. We know we were meant for something beyond the last accomplishment or addition to our resume. We want to know why God created us. We want to go from success in the eyes of the world to significance in the eyes of God. It's about living a life of joy while we're here, and leaving a meaningful legacy when we're gone. The challenge is discovering that kind of purpose.

In fact, recent surveys suggest that up to **97 percent of people never find their true purpose in life**. Most people tend to run full speed on the treadmill of life without taking time to step back and ask the important questions: Who am I? and Why am I here?

success in the eyes of God

Yet, there is proof that the desire for purpose remains strong. For example, Pastor Rick Warren's book *The Purpose Driven Life* is one of the best-selling books of all time. In it, he magnificently describes what we call the "universal or general purpose" of all mankind:

- We were planned for God's pleasure.
- We were formed for God's family.
- We were created to be like Christ.
- We were shaped for serving God.
- We were made for a mission.

But even with a clear understanding of these five very important truths, do you still find yourself wondering how to make it personal? Do you find yourself asking any of these questions?

- How do these universal purposes apply to me?
- How do I know what God has specifically planned for my life?
- How am I meant to serve God and others?
- What am I supposed to "do" and how do I figure it out?

What are the questions that come to mind for you?

OUR EXPERIENCE—OUR PURPOSE

As we searched Scripture, worked with experts, and prayed about these questions, it became clear to us that our purpose goes far beyond our roles and the universal purpose we share with others. We became committed to joining the three percent of people who know their God-given purpose. We wanted to spend our days blessed with focus, peace, and confidence. We wanted to be all we were supposed to be. We wanted to use all we'd been given in the way God intended.

The result of our personal search for answers brought us to a new purpose for our lives: sharing this process of discovering your identity and destiny with people just like you. Through the **7 Steps to Purpose,** we discovered answers for ourselves and we believe that God has directed us to share the process through our Tampa-based coaching practice; our growing team of certified coaches, counselors, consultants, and pastors; and workbooks that can be used by individuals and study groups around the world.

WIIFY: WHAT'S IN IT FOR YOU?

In the weeks ahead, we will help you:

- Find, know, and live your God-given purpose
- Gain the freedom to love yourself just the way God created you
- Experience the tangible day-to-day benefits of a life lived on purpose
- Deepen your relationship with God as you learn to seek His will, listen to His voice, and obey His direction
- Answer God with gratitude and confidence when He asks: "What did you do with all that I gave you?"

You have planted much, but have harvested little.

THE VALUE OF LIVING ON PURPOSE

First, let's take a look at the value of living on purpose and then we'll help you determine how well your daily life is aligned with that. God has given each of us the burning desire for meaning and purpose in life. Let's take a look at a few examples in history to prove that point:

An ancient Greek fable tells the story of Sisyphus, a crafty king who angered Zeus by telling his secrets. He was sentenced to pushing a giant boulder up a steep hill, only to have it roll back down each time it neared the summit. To this day, impossible tasks are called Sisyphean challenges. The Greeks knew that true torture was a life with no purpose.

Haggai, a prophet who lived 500 years before Christ, exhorted the Jews to begin rebuilding the temple in Jerusalem: "You have planted much, but have harvested little. You eat, but never have enough. You drink, but never have your fill. You put on clothes, but are not warm. You earn wages, only to put them in a purse with holes in it." Clearly, this is a view of life without meaning and satisfaction.

More recently, Albert Einstein defined insanity as "doing the same thing over and over again and expecting different results." Insanity is knowing there is more to life but never making the effort to search it out.

All three stories illustrate the critical importance of having purpose. As you will learn through **7 Steps to Purpose**, a well-defined individual purpose brings energy, confidence, and power. Without it, you are likely to struggle with the kind of frustration that results when you lack clear direction and meaning in your life.

ARE YOU LIVING ON PURPOSE?

Before we begin the first series of assessments, let's take a snapshot of where you are now. This simple questionnaire is a quick and easy way to see how you are doing when it comes to living on purpose. Again, there are no "right" or "wrong" answers and we've yet to meet anyone who couldn't improve upon their score as they work through the **7 Steps to Purpose**. Regardless of where you're starting, the goal is to discover your God-given purpose and live a life you truly love. Rank the following statements on a scale of one to five. (We've also posted this questionnaire online in the Resource area at www.IdentityandDestiny.com. We recommend retaking the assessment on a regular basis to ensure that you stay on track with God's purpose for your life.)

PURPOSE QUESTIONNAIRE

(1 = Never True, 5 = Always True)

I wake up on Monday mornings energized and ready for the day.	1 2 3 4 5
I am passionate about my work and/or my role in life.	1 2 3 4 5
I feel a sense of power and confidence in my life and my choices.	1 2 3 4 5
My spiritual life is central to the way I live and the choices I make.	1 2 3 4 5
I know my gifts and strengths and use them in what I do each day.	1 2 3 4 5
I am clear on my core values and beliefs.	1 2 3 4 5
I live my life consistently with those core values and beliefs.	1 2 3 4 5
I am clear about the unique gifts, talents, and experiences that make me who I am.	1 2 3 4 5
I am clear on the things that I am passionate about in my life.	1 2 3 4 5
I know my priorities in life.	1 2 3 4 5
I live my life in harmony with those priorities.	1 2 3 4 5

I am able to maintain a healthy balance between the people, activities, and obligations that are important to me. 1 2 3 4 5

I am certain of my God-given purpose. 1 2 3 4 5

Day-in and day-out, I live my life according to that purpose. 1 2 3 4 5

If asked, I am readily able to articulate the purpose of my life. 1 2 3 4 5

I take time on a regular basis to assess where I am and where I want to be. 1 2 3 4 5

I have a clear understanding of how to move my life forward in alignment with my true purpose. 1 2 3 4 5

I have spent time finding (through prayer, meditation, or self-analysis) the deepest desires of my soul. 1 2 3 4 5

I have a life that is free from fear and frustration. 1 2 3 4 5

I have a life that allows me the freedom to do what I love and I have fun doing it. 1 2 3 4 5

Go back through the exercise and total the number of points you have circled.

Total Score ____________________

Based on your total score, refer to the scoring category below that applies to you:

SCORING FOR THE PURPOSE QUESTIONNAIRE

85-100
Congratulations! It is obvious that you have taken the time to know yourself and have a pretty clear understanding of your purpose. You are living life at a high level of satisfaction, confidence, and peace. Yet, this scorecard can still give you insight into areas where you might be able to improve those blessings. Identify areas where you scored less than five, and keep those points in mind as you work through the **7 Steps to Purpose**. Look for ways you can put the final touches on living a life fully guided by purpose. If your purpose includes sharing those blessings with others, *Identity and Destiny* may be the ideal tool for you to use as a guide in helping others search for purpose.

70-84
Life is good. You have a clear understanding of what you want from life and the skills you bring to the table. You may not be fully aware of your purpose or how to allow it to guide all aspects of your life. There is still unrealized potential. You could easily go from good to great and odds are that you are inclined to make the effort to do so. As you work through the **7 Steps to Purpose**, focus on the areas where you can improve, particularly the spiritual aspects of the program. God has given you many gifts—now is the time to show Him that you are a good steward.

50-69
As you look around at others, you probably feel that you are doing okay. However, you may also find yourself thinking *there must be more to life than this*. You're not certain of your purpose and you probably don't feel as though you are able to live according to the things that matter most. You may find yourself feeling that life is more work than pleasure and you would love to find a way to have a life filled with more purpose, passion, and fun. Living on purpose with God's goals for you will give you that passion. It's also easier to make decisions about priorities and life's questions when you are confident that you are living up to God's expectations for you.

30-49
You're surviving, but life is not giving you the satisfaction that you desire. From time to time, you try to step back and look at yourself and your life, but you've never really been able to pull it all together in a way that gives you clear focus and meaning. You find it difficult to make decisions about life, work, and priorities with real confidence or certainty. Rather than plan and act, you tend to react and just hope for the best. Sometimes it works, sometimes it doesn't. Either way, you are not living your life with a clear understanding of who you are or why you are here. Working through the **7 Steps to Purpose** will help you identify your God-given gifts and then show you how He wants you to use them. You'll be able to maximize your enjoyment, effectiveness, and results in life when you understand why God made you the way He did.

Less than 30
Life simply seems to happen. You don't feel a sense of direction or purpose. Frustration, fatigue, and even a certain level of fear are present in your life most of the time. Either the busyness of life or the struggles and difficulties have prevented you from taking time to think about how you really want to live. You find it hard to clearly define your priorities and even more difficult to live according to what you deem important. We pray that this assessment is the wake-up call you need. As you work through the **7 Steps to Purpose**, you can learn who you are and understand God's purpose for you. Just as importantly, you'll learn to accept that all the events in your life are used by God to build the abilities, attitudes, skills, and character you need to fulfill His purpose for you.

WRAPPING IT UP

The Purpose Scorecard you completed gives a clear indication of how close you are to living "on purpose." Beyond giving you a numerical score, it gives you a baseline measurement of how well you are living the abundant life God desires for you. Ultimately, we all want to live that abundant life God promises to us in John 10:10. But first you must take an honest look at where you are now.

How did you score?

Did your scores surprise you? How and why?

Do you recognize some specific areas for improvement? Elaborate.

List one action step you could take now to begin seeing improvement?

Day 2 | *Welcome*

Yesterday's Purpose Questionnaire was designed to help you answer the question "Am I living on purpose?" Today we're going to talk about the benefits and joy you will discover when you live according to God's plan for your life. We will also take a look at the probable consequences of not living on purpose.

But first, let us share a story to illustrate this point.

THE MILLIONAIRE'S PRAYER

Robert Leatherwood, a development officer for International Cooperating Ministries, typically works with men aged 55 to 75 who have a net worth of more than a million dollars. Most are independent business owners who contribute more than $10,000 a year to help ICM build infrastructure and the hope of Christ in third-world countries.

Over the years, he's built relationships with his donors and often includes their personal needs in his morning prayers. The first two prayer requests are probably no surprise: (1) improved health for themselves and their loved ones, and (2) the lives of their adult children who are struggling or do not have a personal relationship with God.

The third most requested prayer, however, was somewhat of a surprise coming from men who had achieved such worldly success. They asked Robert: "Please pray for me that I might discern what God wants me to do with the rest of my life."

Robert learned that people with great success and wealth still find themselves wanting more out of life. Their desire for purpose and significance haunts them even when the rest of the world thinks they have it all.

This insight led Robert to the *Identity and Destiny* program and he became one of our first Certified Program Leaders. He continues to be an instrumental source of wisdom and encouragement for us and the many clients he has personally coached through the **7 Steps** program.

The desire—and the struggle—to know our purpose is something that challenges most of us in one way or another. Let's press on with the next exercise and find out why!

BENEFITS OF PURPOSE: PART 1

Living without purpose and direction can be a difficult and confusing way to go through life.

Rate each statement on a scale of one to five.
(1 = "almost never," 5 = "nearly constant.")

Fatigue **1 2 3 4 5**
You're always tired and work is a chore. You're pushing against the grain so everything requires extra effort and energy. You lack passion and don't feel connected to the people and things that are important in your life.

Frustration **1 2 3 4 5**
Every obstacle becomes a major problem. Nothing comes easily or smoothly. Everything creates a physical, mental, or emotional drain and you have no sense of accomplishment even at the end of a long day. You feel stuck in life with no hope of ever escaping your problems.

Fear **1 2 3 4 5**
Everything is a challenge and your confidence and self-image are shaken. You are constantly fearful of what might happen next.

Fragmentation **1 2 3 4 5**
You're not connected to what you do on a day-to-day basis. Polls consistently show that only about half of all employees say they are engaged in their jobs. They show up for work and are reasonably productive but they're not passionate about where they spend most of their waking hours. Another 20 percent of people are actively disengaged, physically there but psychologically absent, and generally unhappy about their wasted time. People who don't have jobs outside their homes may feel as though they are simply going through the motions. Nothing has real significance or meaning.

Based on your highest scores above, identify the most significant challenges you are facing. List them below.

BENEFITS OF PURPOSE: PART 2

People who have gained clarity on their individual purpose and live according to God's plans find they can be filled with joy, even as they deal with problems.

Rate each statement on a scale of one to five.
(1 = "almost never," 5 = "nearly constant.")

Energy **1 2 3 4 5**
Life is exciting and you look forward to leaping out of bed in the morning. Challenges actually create energy and passion.

Empowerment **1 2 3 4 5**
You easily overcome problems and feel the synchronicity. Everything seems to work in harmony and in sync because you are in "the zone." Things flow easily and you feel unstoppable.

Confidence **1 2 3 4 5**
You feel sure of your direction and actions. You look forward to challenges because you feel good about yourself.

Focus **1 2 3 4 5**
You have a clearly defined purpose and plumb-line for your decisions. You are able to confidently allocate your time, talent, financial resources, and energy. Living God's purpose reduces doubt and concern as you gain clarity on your best direction and activities.

Fun **1 2 3 4 5**
Life is a pleasure; you laugh easily and live with a sense of play and adventure.

Freedom **1 2 3 4 5**
Knowing who you are and how God "wired" you brings awareness, understanding, and strong self-acceptance. You have the confidence and freedom to be the YOU that God intended.

Commitment **1 2 3 4 5**
With clarity comes commitment. You have confidence in your decisions, so you don't waiver among choices. The sense of providence gives you increased boldness and effectiveness.

Based on your highest scores in Part 2, list the areas where you are experiencing the greatest success.

As you work through the **7 Steps** program, there will be many opportunities to identify ways to have fewer of the challenges in Part 1 and more of the successes in Part 2.

We include this assessment here to highlight the positive change you can expect to see in your life when you complete the **7 Steps to Purpose**. Like everything in life that's worthwhile, it will take some time and effort—but the results will be more than worth it.

When you identify your purpose, you can leave fear, frustration, and fatigue behind. You can experience life the way God fully intended!

I have come that they may have life, and have it to the full. John 10:10

Here are some of the comments we hear from people who have completed the process:

"I no longer feel like a round peg in a square hole."

"Purpose is now my 'plumb line.' My priorities are easier to set. My choices and decisions are easier to make."

"Thankfully, balance and sanity are now the norm rather than the exception in my life."

"Knowing my purpose has given me a power that very few people possess. I have the power to say NO… because my YES is so big!"

"Your program came at the perfect time—I affirmed my purpose, gained greater knowledge of myself, and deepened my relationship with the Lord—thank you so much!"

The benefits of knowing your purpose are real, tangible, and achievable.

WRAPPING IT UP

What is the single most important benefit you hope to gain through the discovery of your God-given purpose?

What do you hope to be able to say when you reach the end of the **7 Steps** program?

Reflecting on Robert Leatherwood's story, what are your top three prayer requests?

We invite you to go to our website (www.IdentityandDestiny.com) and send an email sharing your prayer requests. We would love to join you in prayer for those things in the weeks ahead. You can also sign up on the site for weekly emails that will encourage you as you move through the **7 Steps** program. We hope you will also be commenting on the blog and keeping up with us on Facebook. (You can find all our social media links on the homepage of our website.)

Day 3 | *Welcome*

THERE'S ONLY ONE YOU

The greatest tragedy in life is not death, but a life lived without FINDING, KNOWING, and LIVING your purpose.

As our pastor Matthew Hartsfield of Van Dyke Church in Tampa, Florida often reminds us, the statistical odds on death are still 100 percent. We will all die one day but the hope is that we will meet our Lord in heaven and hear Him say: "Well done, good and faithful servant."

Pastor Matthew encourages us to be devoted to serving others and completing the work God has planned for us while we're here. He compares it to being on a football team: As a player, you have to decide whether you will get into the game and give it your all or hang back on the bench and avoid the "tough stuff" that's out on the field. He says his goal is to arrive in heaven completely used up with grass stains all over his jersey. He wants to be able to say, "Lord, I was fearless in your name. I left skin in the game!" Wow! What a way to look at life and your God-given purpose. Live it with gusto and excitement. No fear. No reservation.

If you're like we are, you're anxious to hear God say: "Well done." But to do that, we believe you must find your purpose and live it! You must understand that God has created only one you and He has a very specific purpose that ONLY you can fulfill.

It is clear to us, friends, that God not only loves you very much but also has put his hand on you for something special. 1 Thessalonians 1:4 (TM)

Yes, He has something special for each of you! Now, please carefully consider what we are about to say:

- In the entire world, there is only one you.
- You are fearfully and wonderfully made.
- God formed you with His hands and loves you with all His heart.
- There is no one who will ever duplicate or replace you.
- Your life is meant for a purpose, and
- You are uniquely designed by God to accomplish that purpose.

But, as Pastor Matthew would say: "Will you get in the game? Will you give it your all?"

You may not be ready to answer those questions quite yet, but odds are you are doing this study because there are times when you found yourself thinking,

Yes, I want to live my purpose, but here's the problem: I don't know what it is and I don't know how to find it!

That is exactly why we believe God helped us design and develop this program. Between today and tomorrow we will lay out your plan of action for the weeks ahead. We will give you an overview of the **7 Steps to Purpose** and show you how to go directly to God for answers.

One of the cornerstones of the program is this: If you want to know why you were created, ask your Creator!

If any of you lacks wisdom, he should ask God who gives generously to all without finding fault. James 1:5

SEEK AND YOU WILL FIND

We believe...God is sincere about His promises. As it says in ***Matthew 7:7: Ask and it will be given.*** If you want to know your purpose, ask God. Sincerely seek Him for the answers, and He will respond.

We believe...God is NOT going to make this a guessing game. You may have to exercise patience and perseverance, but He clearly wants you to discover your purpose and rejoice in the benefits that go along with it.

We believe...God wants your participation. It takes desire and it takes action. If you do your part by diligently following the **7 Steps** program—without fail—we have seen God do His part. That is why you will often hear us say:

You do the Steps—God does the Rest!

God is not going to make this a guessing game

THE 7 STEPS: AN OVERVIEW

Our early work with the **7 Steps to Purpose** was based on direct coaching with individuals and small groups as we shared our vision for how God reveals His plans to each individual who prayerfully asks and seeks. As we have continued to refine the program, we've drawn from hundreds of coaching sessions—plus years of studying Scripture, wisdom from our spiritual mentors, and our own personal experiences seeking the Lord and discovering our purpose.

With God's blessing and direction, we have created this seven-step process that goes far beyond the many "purpose" programs that simply take you through a few intellectual assessments and quickly have you writing personal mission statements. With the **7 Steps to Purpose**, that is just the beginning. We start with intellectual exploration because it is an important part of the process.

But there is so much more to be learned. The latter steps of this program focus on allowing God to be an instrumental part of the process. As we said earlier, the core belief that undergirds this program is based on spending time seeking the Lord and directly requesting His insight and answers.

In **Steps 1 to 3**, you'll take a look at the "real" you to identify your strengths, resilience, and personal style using tests and techniques proven in both spiritual and secular settings. You'll also use questionnaires that help you define your core beliefs and passions. You'll be able to identify your God-given talents and abilities along with the communication systems and people skills that you've developed over your lifetime.

Step 1: How Are You Wired? — Personality Style and Resilience
Step 2: What Makes You Tick? — Core Values and Spiritual Gifts
Step 3: What's Your Passion? — Passion Pursuit

Step 4 is the "bridge," where you'll take a look at any limiting beliefs, fears, or blocks that may be preventing you from knowing and living your God-given purpose. Acknowledging these, and then connecting with the Lord to work through them, will allow you to move past any potential roadblocks and into a deeper level of investigating your purpose.

In **Steps 5 to 7**, we'll use five distinct spiritual disciplines. It is in these final three steps that you turn from self-analysis and begin to seek the Lord directly for answers about your purpose. In this phase, we will help you clearly define your **identity, destiny,** and **assignment.** You will be asking the Lord for what we call ESV:

- Elaboration on what He has shown you in earlier steps.
- Specification and details on the things He is showing you.
- Validation and confirmation that you are on the right track and can trust what you are being given.

Step 5: Can You Hear God Speaking? — Dreams, Prayers, and Meditation
Step 6: Can You Be Still and Listen? — Listening Prayer and Dialogue Journaling
Step 7: Who Am I? and Why Am I Here? — Creating Your Purpose Statements

Nearly everyone who completes the process comes to a breakthrough moment in this final phase when they realize they've truly found their purpose. Almost without exception, there is a profound level of physiological and emotional response to this discovery which is truly life altering!

WRAPPING IT UP

Do you believe God created you for something special? Explain.

Are you ready to find and live the purpose God has for your life? Explain.

Is there anything standing in the way of living your life's purpose? Explain.

Describe a time when you had to "step out in faith" and it was only then that everything else seemed to fall into place.

Day 4 | *Welcome*

THE THREE ELEMENTS OF PURPOSE

In developing the *Identity and Destiny* process, we've discovered three separate elements of purpose: your **identity, destiny,** and **assignment**. We will use the terms frequently and want you to have a clear understanding of what we mean by each of them:

Element 1: Identity
Identity is NOT what you do but who you are. It is a presence you exude from your very core. It is a feeling or a quality of being.

Experience shows that the Lord gives you identity clues throughout your life, but you may not have been aware of them. As you work through the program, we will help you look at your past, as well as the new things you are learning, to see how they point to your identity.

Your identity statement will complete the sentence "I am ____________," but it goes far beyond ego, pride, or desire. It is God-given, soul-deep, and resonates from within.

Your identity statement will be your anchor. It will bring you back to the place where you first said, "Yes, that's it!" It will put into words God's description of what He sees in you and who you are in His eyes. This will likely be the first time many of you receive such profound insight and blessing directly from your Creator.

Element 2: Destiny
Destiny is what you do, but it is NOT your job or career. It's just you being you. It does not matter what job, task, or role you are engaged in, your destiny has the power to be revealed and lived out in everything you do. We like to say: "Your destiny is an expression of God's Spirit working in the world through you."

Spend a moment thinking that through. How would you change your life if you knew that everything you did was a reflection of God and His plan for your life?

As you move forward, keep this in mind: Your identity and destiny statements aren't meant to be used like corporate taglines or marketing statements for a brand. They're between you and the Lord. If you go through this workbook on your own instead of in a study group, you may rarely voice them to another human being. The purpose is to internalize your identity and destiny until they become your own. It is about truly beginning to see yourself as God sees you. Then you will not just **find** and **know** your purpose, but **live** it every moment of every day!

Once you get to the end of the process, you will have time to "wordsmith" your purpose statements and determine how and when you will share them. But for now, we just want you to hear directly from God on the matter. The most important thing is for you to allow God to bring your purpose to your conscious mind and speak a blessing of purpose into your life.

Your purpose statements have the ability to become your guidance system. They become a God-given compass for the choices you make, the work you do, and the way you serve others. And one thing we have recognized with certainty: God's purpose always transcends self!

Element 3: Assignment
Assignment is a specific God-given task to be performed. It can go far beyond or be in addition to your current job or career. It is what the Lord is asking you to do next. Your assignment may or may not be what you had in mind when you first started the program. You may want answers in one area and God seems to be talking about everything but that. Be patient. He may be telling you there are other things that need to be accomplished first. He may be saying the time is not right. He may know that you have some growing to do. Whatever it is, our best advice is listen, obey, and simply do what He is asking. It will ultimately lead you to joy and purpose as He accomplishes His will in your life.

purpose
always
transcends
self

Also, bear in mind it is rare that God will lay out all the details of His plan for your life at once. God wants relationship. He wants you looking to Him for strength and guidance. He knows what needs to happen next to prepare you. He knows that you might be prone to take matters into your own hands. He knows what is best and will give you the right assignment but no more. He will add to it when He is ready and—more importantly—when He knows you are ready.

The nature of an assignment is very different from identity and destiny. Your identity and destiny tell you who you are and why you are here. Assignments are tasks—things you must choose to act on. You may have one, complete it, and then go for months or even years before God gives you another. Your assignment is usually the last of the three elements of purpose to be revealed, and it's often the most exciting, yet scariest, element of all. It may be something you can't wait to grab hold of, or it may require significant change in your life. It could present an apparently insurmountable challenge or you could say: "Bring it on, Lord, I'm ready."

Either way, don't be discouraged. You can rest assured that God knows best. You can trust His sovereign plan and timing. Just take a look in Scripture for encouragement. God often takes ordinary people and gives them amazing assignments. Biblical leaders like Abraham, Moses, Gideon, and the apostles were all given extraordinary tasks.

Some, like Moses and Abraham, had to be groomed through years of preparation before they were allowed to begin. Others, like the apostles, were called with no warning or preparation at all. Some, like Peter and Matthew, dropped everything and went directly into their assignments. Then others, like Gideon and Moses, had to be coaxed and cajoled into the assignment that God lay before them.

Take a look at your own life. Can you see how there have been life events, experiences, and opportunities that have allowed you to grow and be prepared for the things you are doing now? Other people may not see it, or they may think of you as an "an overnight success," but you know better. In all likelihood, there's been hard work, hard knocks, and perseverance required to get *where* you are today. And the same applies to *who* you are!

what God starts, no man can stop

As you work through this program, you will be given various opportunities to look back over your life and identify the things that have shaped you. It will be an important part of understanding all that God has planned for your life. And rest assured, He is still in the business of using the whole of your life for His plans. The good, the bad, the ugly, and the beautiful: He weaves it all together for our good and His glory!

OUR ASSIGNMENT

In many ways, the fact that you have this workbook in your hands is the perfect example of how God can make people rethink even their best-laid plans. We have both been entrepreneurs for most of our lives, but several years ago God clearly called us away from our comfort zones in corporate America to become coaches who help individuals discover their purpose in life. To further complicate matters, He began making it obvious that we could reach far more people through the written word than one-on-one or small group sessions.

As God began to put that idea in our hearts and minds, to be honest, we struggled with it. We reminded God that the only book we had ever authored was a technical manual on business valuation. But somehow He seemed to be saying that was all He needed. God knew that by combining our backgrounds in corporate and strategic planning with our coaching expertise, He could use us if we were willing. So we slowly began putting one foot in front of the other.

We both were involved in small groups at the time, and we especially enjoyed having a workbook to follow as we did our Bible studies. Drawing on that experience, God said, "Take the **7 Steps** program and create a workbook that you would like to use." He even lined up some of our spiritual mentors who suggested the same thing—with no prompting from us. It was just the confirmation we needed. We looked at all that was happening and took it to mean that God was serious about this assignment and we had better get to work.

What God starts, no man can stop. We are just glad that we did not turn our back on this awesome opportunity to serve God and all who will benefit from what we have written.

WRAPPING IT UP

Based on what you learned today, write your own personal definition of the three elements of purpose:

Identity:

Destiny:

Assignment:

Reflecting on our story about writing this workbook, describe a time when you can see you were prepared for an assignment only because of other, seemingly unrelated, experiences in your past.

List events and circumstances from your past that you think may have shaped who you are today. Think of both the good and the bad. Remember: He weaves it ALL together for good.

Day 5 | Welcome

YOUR PURPOSE MOSAIC

In many ways, working through the **7 Steps to Purpose** is like creating a mosaic. As you go through the process, you'll learn a great deal about yourself. Through a creative series of questionnaires and assessments, you will take an in-depth look at the unique strengths and abilities God has blessed you with.

While some of you may have completed inventories like the ones you'll take in the upcoming weeks, we have found very few people who have been able to compile the multi-faceted profile that emerges through the **7 Step** process. On their own, the results of these assessments are like pieces of glass in a mosaic. When an artist first starts the process of building a mosaic, he begins by collecting all the different elements needed for his work of art and arranges the material in groups. The red stones, the green glass, the brown pebbles, the blue painted bits of clay—they all are gathered and sorted into similar groupings. Then, when it is time to actually create the mosaic, all the separate pieces are artfully placed together to compose the finished masterpiece.

Like pieces of glass in a mosaic, the individual assessments measure only a small part of the unique "YOU" that God has created. As we near the end of the program, we will help you gather those pieces, sort them, and then create your masterpiece. This workbook includes many places for you to journal and record your findings as you work through the **7 Steps to Purpose**. Daily "wrapping it up" sessions are designed to help you summarize and organize your findings on a day-by-day basis followed by weekly reviews to pinpoint the most important things you've learned. As we mentioned earlier, there will be many discoveries and insights as you work the program. If you wait until the conclusion, it will be impossible to recapture all the thoughts, feelings, and revelations that have come to you along the way.

God

inspired

self-portrait

Use these sections, as well as the intentionally wide margins throughout the book, to record the words, phrases, pictures, feelings, concepts, and key thoughts that have come from your week's work. As we near the end of the process, you'll collate and organize that information. For now, the goal will be to capture the essence of what you are discovering.

When you get to the end of the process, we will help you arrange the information and put the final touches on your God-inspired self-portrait. When all the pieces come together, your identity, destiny, and purpose will become clear. This final composition is a powerful masterpiece that answers two questions that will change your life forever:

In the eyes of God, my Creator: Who am I? and Why am I here?

THE FINAL TOUCHES

The first week of our journey is almost complete; it just needs a few finishing touches.

The final exercise today will introduce the weekly review, a task you will be completing at the end of each week designed to summarize the best of what you've discovered.

First, we will list a few highlights from the past week. Then, in a section called **My Big "Aha"**, we'll ask you to add your own personal highlights. There will also be a spot called **Capture It** where you can collect pieces for your mosaic: thoughts, words, pictures, and feelings you don't want to forget. We will finish with some time in **Scripture** and leave a space for any additional journaling or notes you want to record.

Review | *Welcome*

KEY POINTS TO REMEMBER!

- You are unique, special, and handcrafted by God.
- Only you can fulfill the purpose God has planned for your life.
- Your Identity resonates from deep within; it is who you are at the core.
- Your Destiny is an expression of God's spirit working in the world through you.
- Finding your purpose allows you to experience life the way God intended: abundantly!
- Knowing your purpose gives you a plumb line. It gives you the power to say "No" because your "Yes" is so big.
- If you want to know your purpose, ask God, sincerely seek His wisdom, and He will gladly tell you.
- Finding your purpose is a process, like creating a mosaic. Enjoy the journey.
- You do the Steps—God does the Rest!

My Big "Aha"
List the most dramatic and important things you discovered or learned this week.

Capture It!
Go back through Week 1 and record the words, phrases, pictures, feelings, concepts, and key thoughts that have come from this week's work.

God's Word
Identify the Scripture that impacted you most deeply this week and journal your thoughts in the following format:

First, write out the Scripture:

Secondly, identify its **Message** to you:

Then **Apply** it to your life:

Finally, write a **Prayer** back to God about this Scripture. Thank Him, ask for help, or just talk about it with Him, whatever feels right.

Personal Notes, Thoughts, and Journaling

STEP 1 | WEEK TWO

How Are You Wired?

PERSONALITY STYLE ANALYSIS

RESILIENCE QUOTIENT

Day 1 | *How Are You Wired?*

PERSONALITY STYLE ANALYSIS

Today we begin Step 1—the first step in the "intellectual phase" of the **7 Steps to Purpose.** In the coming three weeks, you will work through five unique assessments. Each is designed to help you learn more about who you are and how God "wired" you. You will discover your:

- primary personality style
- resilience quotient
- top five core values
- dominant spiritual gift
- strongest passions—and the needs that drive them.

You will explore your likes and dislikes along with your strengths and passion. You will zero in on the things that drive and inspire you. You will look at people, events, and circumstances that have shaped the person you are today. You will identify areas where you can bolster your ability to overcome adversity, and begin to recognize all the Lord has generously given to help you realize your dreams and goals. As with the apostle Paul, we hope you will not only recognize your gifts but also see God as the provider of them:

At the moment I have all I need—and more! I am generously supplied with the gifts you sent me. Philippians 4:18

You will learn more about the five assessments as you proceed through the program. But, with each one, remember our analogy of a mosaic. Each time you review your findings and results, you are collecting important pointers toward your God-given purpose. You are learning how the Lord has uniquely crafted and designed you. No single piece of information will provide the full answer. Each provides an important element of the overall purpose the Lord wants to reveal and a separate piece of the mosaic you are building. Don't jump to conclusions. Enjoy each exercise and recognize the valuable information being provided about you and your purpose.

As you proceed, rest assured there are no right or wrong answers for any of these assessments. The goal is self-awareness and acceptance—not pass or fail! The tools you will be using have proven effective in corporate settings for more than 50 years and are combined with those we've developed specifically for the *Identity and Destiny* process. Businesses use assessments like these to help determine how effective an employee will be in achieving corporate goals. In the **7 Steps to Purpose**, you will be using them to highlight what the Lord has given you, and ultimately, to help you find, know, and live your God-given purpose.

Remember: The Lord is your Creator. You are fearfully and wonderfully made, and He has a wonderful plan and purpose for your life. Your job is to discover it.

You do the steps—God does the rest!

DISC: THE LANGUAGE OF BEHAVIOR

fearfully

and

wonderfully

made

Now, let's get started with your Personality Style Analysis. It's known as a DISC profile and is based on the pioneering work of Harvard psychologist William Moulton Marston. In his 1928 book on the subject, he describes four classic quadrants of human behavior:

D = Dominant, Driver
I = Influencing, Inspiring
S = Steady, Stable
C = Correct, Compliant

The DISC is often referred to as the "language of behavior." Knowing your strongest behavior quadrant will help you know your language and understand yourself better. As it relates to purpose, it will help you recognize the roles you are best suited to fill and those that simply aren't a good fit. It is not that you are incapable of doing certain things or exhibiting all four characteristics of DISC. Odds are, you can do anything you put your mind to. But, the critical questions you will answer here are:

- How am I naturally wired to behave?
- What's my behavioral comfort zone?

You will learn the basic motivation that drives your behavior, your best situations and environments, and your best way of communicating, interacting with others, and making decisions.

Here is an important thought to bear in mind as you explore the various types of personalities: It takes ALL the styles to make good families, marriages, teams, churches, small groups, and organizations. The greatest value of knowing your personality style—and that of others—is to recognize, understand, and appreciate the differences!

For as we have many members in one body, but all the members do not have the same function, so we, being many, are one body in Christ, and individually members of one another. Romans 12:4-5

DISC PERSONALITY STYLE ANALYSIS

For more than three decades, this 24-question profile has proven highly accurate in revealing your primary personality style. It will reveal much about your communication style, the way you make decisions, and the way you prefer to work with others.

Step 1: On each of the 24 rows, two options are offered. For each of the 24 rows, circle the option that BEST describes your preferred work style.

	A	B	C	D
1	Gather data, analyze all options carefully	Find creative solutions and promote your favorite one		
2		Find creative solutions and promote your favorite one	Act decisively without second-guessing	
3			Act decisively without second-guessing	Seek consensus, be diplomatic
4	Gather data, analyze all options carefully		Act decisively without second-guessing	
5		Find creative solutions and promote your favorite one		Seek consensus, be diplomatic
6	Gather data, analyze all options carefully			Seek consensus, be diplomatic
7	Conscientious, loyal, adhere to rules	Enthusiastic, cheerful		
8		Enthusiastic, cheerful	Assertive, question the status quo	
9			Assertive, question the status quo	Dependable, warm, friendly, prefer status quo
10	Conscientious, loyal, adhere to rules		Assertive, question the status quo	
11		Enthusiastic, cheerful		Dependable, warm, friendly, prefer status quo
12	Conscientious, loyal, adhere to rules			Dependable, warm, friendly, prefer status quo
13	Structured, quality-driven	Persuasive, optimistic		
14		Persuasive, optimistic	Direct, competitive	
15			Direct, competitive	Patient, steady
16	Structured, quality-driven		Direct, competitive	
17		Persuasive, optimistic		Patient, steady
18	Structured, quality-driven			Patient, steady
19	Seek accuracy	Gain social recognition		
20		Gain social recognition	Achieve results	
21			Achieve results	Be dependable, stable
22	Seek accuracy		Achieve results	
23		Gain social recognition		Patient, steady
24	Seek accuracy			Patient, steady

Step 2: Score the assessment by counting the number of responses you circled in each column and write the totals in the boxes below.
The sum of the totals should be 24.

	A	B	C	D
Total				

Now, let's translate these scores into your **DISC score**:

Your **D** is the score in box C above—write that score here: ______

Your **I** is the score in box B above—write that score here: ______

Your **S** is the score in box D above—write that score here: ______

Your **C** is the score in box A above—write that score here: ______

Step 3: Graph your DISC profile. Transfer the numbers you have just written on the four lines above, marking the score in the appropriate column below. If the score for your D is 9, put a dot in the box across from 9 in the column marked D. Do this in all four columns. The final step is to connect the dots to create your DISC line graph.

	D	I	S	C
12				
11				
10				
9				
8				
7				
6				
5				
4				
3				
2				
1				
0				

As you look at your scores and the graph you just created, what is the character trait with the highest score? Which of the four styles—D, I, S, or C—is plotted at the highest point on your graph?

This is your dominant personality style.

LET'S HAVE SOME FUN

Our good friend and DISC expert Joe Matthews, president and founder of the Franchise Performance Group, has typecast the four personality styles as characters. Have fun as you get to know these characters and gain valuable insight into each personality style:

The D is "The Action Hero." They are outgoing, hard-charging, risk-taking, efficient, disciplined, organized, and results-oriented. They are take-charge characters! They make gut-based decisions rather than logical or information-based decisions. Attaining goals and achieving results drives them. They speak pointedly and directly, "telling it like it is." They possess strong opinions and are often closed to any new facts that contradict their formed opinions. They have difficulty listening to details and want the bottom line. Since they are such strong personalities, they can easily bowl over weaker personality types if they aren't careful. They are known to resist processes and systems that they did not create. However, they will follow a system if they see it as an efficient method of achieving a result. They resist being told what to do but gravitate toward win-win strategic alliances that achieve results.

Famous Action Heroes: Bill O'Reilly, Hillary Clinton, Bobby Knight, George Patton (and on a more personal level...Tom Wolf).

The I is "The Comedian." They are fun-loving, outgoing, empathetic, risk-taking, people-oriented, charming, affable, creative, enthusiastic, talkative, optimistic, trusting, and highly influential characters. Like the Action Hero, they rely on gut-based decisions but are more people-oriented than task-oriented. Building quality relationships, having fun, and attaining social recognition drives them. Comedians look for reasons to believe in, trust, and like others. They listen more attentively to headlines and highlights rather than all the details. They have trouble saying "no" and have a tendency to over-promise. They prefer to create powerful relationships rather than work alone. They move toward teamwork, synergy, and getting results through people.

Famous Comedians: Robin Williams, Chi Chi Rodriquez, Eddie Murphy (and again on a more personal level...Pam Wolf).

The S is "The Faithful Sidekick." They are warm, dependable, good-natured, structured, methodical, systems-oriented, open-minded, consistent, persistent, level-headed, pragmatic, objective, sincere, and empathetic team players. They are people-oriented, but unlike Comedians, they are more introverted and less emotional. They are driven by the need for security, stability, and belonging. They make slow and informed decisions rather than quick emotional decisions. They are known to be highly detailed, organized, slow-paced, and patient. They are the best listeners and easiest to get along with of all the four characters. They prefer predictable environments and are often risk-averse and resistant to change.

Famous Faithful Sidekicks: Gandhi, Mother Theresa, Mr. Rogers, and Leave it to Beaver's *Ward Cleaver.*

The C is "The Private Eye." They are precise, exact, focused, detailed, neat, systematic, polite, logical, professional, open-minded. and slow-paced. They are the most analytical, compliant, and methodical of the four charters. They are driven by an internal need for perfection and want clear instructions about what is expected of them. They are task-oriented and once they are clear about what is expected, they become self-directed. They are introverted and prefer to work alone. They pride themselves in pouring over information and analyzing data prior to making any type of decision. They need more detail and information than the other three characters before being able to make a decision. They are risk-averse, the least entrepreneurial, and the most resistant to change.

Famous Private Eyes: Felix Unger, Columbo, and Mister Spock.

Taking a look at the character representing your primary personality style should give you a good overview of your preferred style of communication and behavior. This is a good first step in gaining strong self-awareness.

A careful review of the remaining styles will also show you how others tend to operate, and as Steven Covey says in his book *The Seven Habits of Highly Effective People*, "Seek first to understand, then to be understood."

Understanding the personality style of others is a good place to start!

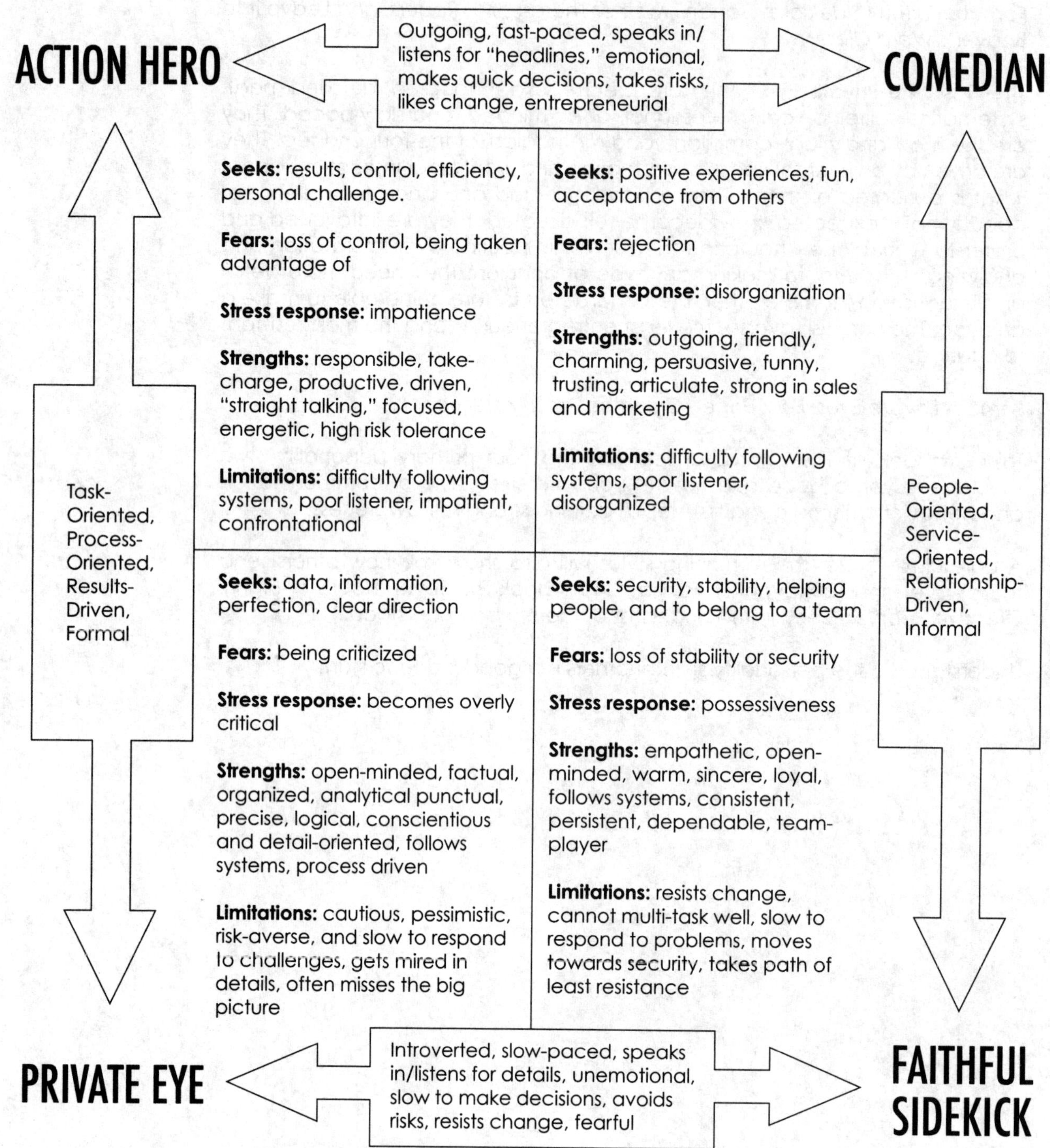
ACTION HERO
Outgoing, fast-paced, speaks in/listens for "headlines," emotional, makes quick decisions, takes risks, likes change, entrepreneurial
COMEDIAN
Task-Oriented, Process-Oriented, Results-Driven, Formal
Seeks: results, control, efficiency, personal challenge.
Fears: loss of control, being taken advantage of
Stress response: impatience
Strengths: responsible, take-charge, productive, driven, "straight talking," focused, energetic, high risk tolerance
Limitations: difficulty following systems, poor listener, impatient, confrontational
Seeks: positive experiences, fun, acceptance from others
Fears: rejection
Stress response: disorganization
Strengths: outgoing, friendly, charming, persuasive, funny, trusting, articulate, strong in sales and marketing
Limitations: difficulty following systems, poor listener, disorganized
People-Oriented, Service-Oriented, Relationship-Driven, Informal
Seeks: data, information, perfection, clear direction
Fears: being criticized
Stress response: becomes overly critical
Strengths: open-minded, factual, organized, analytical punctual, precise, logical, conscientious and detail-oriented, follows systems, process driven
Limitations: cautious, pessimistic, risk-averse, and slow to respond to challenges, gets mired in details, often misses the big picture
Seeks: security, stability, helping people, and to belong to a team
Fears: loss of stability or security
Stress response: possessiveness
Strengths: empathetic, open-minded, warm, sincere, loyal, follows systems, consistent, persistent, dependable, team-player
Limitations: resists change, cannot multi-task well, slow to respond to problems, moves towards security, takes path of least resistance
PRIVATE EYE
Introverted, slow-paced, speaks in/listens for details, unemotional, slow to make decisions, avoids risks, resists change, fearful
FAITHFUL SIDEKICK

WRAPPING IT UP

What is your primary or dominant characteristic: D, I, S, or C?

Based on the descriptors for that characteristic, underline or highlight the two words that describe that trait.

D = Dominant, Driver
I = Influencing, Inspiring
S = Steady, Stable
C = Correct, Compliant

Based on Joe Matthews' descriptions, which character are you?

D = The Action Hero
I = The Comedian
S = The Faithful Sidekick
C = The Private Eye

Based on your dominant character type go back through todays work and list the traits that most accurately describe you.

Accuracy is Often Amazing
We have rarely had anyone say the primary trait identified through the DISC profile is inaccurate. However, if you have doubts, we encourage you to ask the opinion of those who know you best. Sometimes we are not able to see ourselves as clearly as those we live and work with.

Tomorrow, we will provide more detail about each of these personality styles to help bring additional insight and greater understanding.

If you are like the vast majority of people who complete this DISC profile, you're probably rather amazed that these few questions could capture the essence of your personality so well.

Day 2 | How Are You Wired?

PERSONALITY STYLE ANALYSIS

Now that you've completed your DISC profile, you have identified your primary personality style.

Again, what is your dominant characteristic: D, I, S, or C?

Your Primary Style
This trait is your basic or natural personality style. We all have elements of the four styles in our personalities, but this is the one with the strongest influence. It is the behavior mode in which you are most comfortable. It is also your default mode under stress.

As with all the exercises, assessments, and tools in the **7 Steps to Purpose**, the DISC profile is—most importantly—about self-awareness and acceptance. There is no one style that is better than another. It takes all of us, with all the various styles, to accomplish what the Lord has planned. Some will lead, some will follow. Some will see the big picture, others will take care of the details. Some will be on the front lines, others will work behind the scenes. It takes everyone! And besides, wouldn't the world be a boring place if we were all alike?

It is interesting to note that your basic profile will rarely change. If your highest score today is "D," even 20 years from now, that will still be your primary style. Some studies have shown that deeply traumatic life experiences can alter your primary style, but this is definitely not the norm.

Your basic personality is what we call "factory installed." The intensity of the factors may change but your primary style is foundational—it is how you are wired. In Psalm 139, the Lord says you are "fearfully and wonderfully made," and that includes your personality style. The Lord has a plan for you and He has wired you perfectly for that purpose.

Take a look at the chart below to learn more about your primary style. While you are at it, you may also find it interesting to try identifying the styles of others who are important in your life: your spouse, friends, children, boss, or co-workers.

Summary of the Four DISC Personality Styles

	D: Dominant	I: Influencing	S: Steady	C: Compliant
Seeks	Control	Recognition	Acceptance	Accuracy
Strengths	Administration Leadership Determination	Persuading Enthusiasm Entertaining	Listening Teamwork Follow-Through	Planning Systems Orchestration
Challenges	Impatient Insensitive Poor Listener	Lack of Detail Short Attention Low Follow-Through	Oversensitive Slow to Begin Dislikes Change	Perfectionist Critical Unresponsive
Dislikes	Inefficiency Indecision	Routines Complexity	Insensitivity Impatience	Disorganization Impropriety
Decisions	Decisive	Spontaneous	Conferring	Methodical

Do you recognize yourself? Explain.

Do you recognize anyone else you know? Elaborate.

What can you learn from this exercise that might be helpful?

DIVE DEEPER

Want to learn more about your personality style?

A more comprehensive DISC profile is available. By purchasing and completing our full Personality Style Analysis, you will gain access to the same test that has been given to more than 40 million people over the last 30 years. This detailed assessment provides more about your personality profile and gives valuable insight for improving all your important relationships through better understanding and communication. It will increase self–awareness and help you identify your best approach for processing information, making decisions, and producing optimum results.

This online assessment is quick and easy. The results will be returned via email and you can quickly begin learning how to:

- Identify your strengths
- Know yourself better

- Recognize areas of "style adaptation" stress
- Enhance communication with others
- Strengthen relationship skills
- Accelerate personal growth

We encourage everyone to take this step and Dive Deeper. Learn more by visiting the Resources area at www.IdentityandDestiny.com.

As Tom often says, "If I'd begun understanding all that DISC could teach me at 22 rather than 32, I would have saved myself 10 years of trial and error to learn the same thing!"

RECOGNIZING OTHER STYLES

There is much to be learned by knowing your own style and then being able to discern the styles of others. If you are able to correctly identify the style of another person and adapt your style to be more responsive, you will be amazed how much it improves communication and the quality of your relationships.

In the following excerpt from Joe Matthew's book *Developing Peak Performing Franchisees,* he shares how you can quickly predict someone's primary personality style:

> "The best way to predict someone's style is to run their profile. However, running reports isn't always practical and you may need to do a 'quick read' on the fly. The best way to read on the fly is by observing the person you are speaking to and asking yourself the following two questions:
>
> 1. Is the person more outgoing and expressive or introverted and reserved?
>   - Outgoing and expressive are either Comedians or Action Heroes
>   - Introverted and reserved are Faithful Sidekicks or Private Eyes.
> 2. If the person is outgoing and expressive, ask yourself: "Are they more informal and personal or more distant and professional?"
>   - Outgoing, expressive, informal, and personal are Comedians.
>   - Outgoing, expressive, distant, and professional are Action Heroes.
> 3. If you determine the person is introverted and reserved, stop right there. Chances are you aren't going to get any additional cues because they are not expressive. Since 80 percent of introverts are measured to be Faithful Sidekicks,

go with the odds and assume you are dealing with a Sidekick. Sidekicks and Private Eyes are very similar, so it is not that important to make this distinction.

RESPECT AND ADAPT

Once you learn to recognize the dominant personality traits of others, respect for the other person's style is the key! With respect, you can focus on the many benefits of the difference rather than locking onto the annoyances.

We have used the DISC profile in our businesses and coaching practice for over 25 years and learned much about the use of this assessment. We have become so familiar recognizing the four personality styles "on the fly" that we often find ourselves describing someone using the DISC behavioral language. It's funny how we will both be coming home from a social or business gathering and comparing notes on the primary personality styles of people we have just met. It's not only fun and interesting, but proves very useful in knowing how to connect, build rapport, and communicate.

You also can learn to do this. Simply learn to use Joe Matthews's list of questions and his process of elimination. It really does work!

learn to adapt your behavior and meet the needs of others

We also believe there is much to be learned about proper adaptation to the personality styles of others by looking at the example of Jesus. If you study Scripture with this in mind, you will see that Christ is the perfect blend of all four personality types. With the Pharisees, He often exercised His "D." He was definitely the "Action Hero" when He spoke with the dominance and strength those situations often required. Take a look at Matthew 12:25-37 where Jesus refers to the Pharisees as "a brood of vipers." These are strong words, but exactly what was needed in that circumstance.

Then, you can also see how Jesus was more than capable of altering His approach when addressing those who were open and receptive to hearing His message. He would put on the sensitivity and care of the "S" or "Faithful Sidekick"' and speak as He did in John 10:14-5:

I am the good shepherd; I know my sheep and my sheep know me—just as the Father knows me and I know the Father—and I lay down my life for my sheep.

When thinking of the remaining two styles, you can see those exhibited as well. Jesus often used His "I" as He adeptly influenced and persuaded others. Then you can also see His "C" in His compliance to the will of the Father.

Can you think of examples in Scripture that reflect Jesus' ability to adapt His personality to fit the situation? Journal your thoughts as you contemplate the Lord's amazing ability to do this for each and every one of us—always relating to us in just the right way.

We can all take a lesson from the Lord and learn to adapt our behavior and meet the needs of others. Using these skills, you can learn to interact in ways that model the example of Jesus and reflect the fruit of the Spirit.

But the fruit of the Spirit is love, joy, peace, patience, kindness, goodness, faithfulness, gentleness and self-control. Galatians 5:22

OPPOSITES ATTRACT

As you continue to learn about personality styles, you may also find yourself thinking this must be the Lord's way of playing a funny trick on you. Let us ask this: As you look at your closest relationships, do you find yourself thinking there is a lot of truth to the old saying, "opposites attract?" We would suggest that is all part of the Lord's perfect plan. He uses others—especially those with whom we are most intimate—as part of our growth, refinement, and maturity.

together we are able

Take the two of us as an example. Tom is a very strong D and Pam is a high I. Tom likes you to be direct and get to the point, while Pam loves to chat, ask questions, and get to know you personally. Tom is all about getting the job done—putting tasks over people. Pam will often be found putting relationships and people above the task. As you might guess, this makes for a good team, but it also presents some interesting challenges and opportunities to adapt, learn, and grow.

As iron sharpens iron, so one man sharpens another. Proverbs 27:17

In addition to refinement, the Lord also designs and brings us together for our mutual strength and protection. He guides us into relationships knowing that together we are able to do what alone we cannot.

Though one may be overpowered, two can defend themselves. A cord of three strands is not quickly broken. Ecclesiastes 4:12

GOD'S BEST

Learning to adapt, learning to communicate, and learning to respond to the needs of others—it is all part of the work the Lord is doing to help you be your best you. It may even be His way of using other people to help you take the focus off yourself and put it onto God and others. As you begin to learn about the gifts the Lord has given you, it is good to keep in mind that He blesses us so we can bless others. The Lord is all about the flow of gifts and blessings—never about hoarding.

Each of you must bring a gift in proportion to the way the LORD your God has blessed you. Deuteronomy 16:7

And without a doubt the lesser person is blessed by the greater. Hebrews 7:7

Remember, the beginning of self-acceptance is self-awareness and the beginning of all wisdom is fear (trust and respect) of the Lord. (See Proverbs 1:7).

It is a wise person who takes the time to understand themselves and then carefully use the gifts they have been given. The operative word here is *carefully*. As you learn more about your primary style, bear in mind that any trait, taken to an extreme, can be hurtful—to you and others. (To gain more insight on the cautions for each personality type, go back and look at the challenges described in the DISC chart we introduced earlier today).

Good friend, take to heart what I'm telling you; collect my counsels and guard them with your life. Tune your ears to the world of Wisdom; set your heart on a life of Understanding. That's right—if you make Insight your priority, and won't take no for an answer, Searching for it like a prospector panning for gold, like an adventurer on a treasure hunt, Believe me, before you know it Fear-of-God will be yours; you'll have come upon the Knowledge of God. Proverbs 2:1-3 (TM)

Seek understanding and wisdom, fear the Lord, and use your gifts wisely!

WRAPPING IT UP

Thinking of your dominant personality style from DISC, what new understandings did you gain today?

How does the example of Jesus—and His ability to adapt His style—challenge you?

Now that you understand your dominant personality style and those of other people, can you think of a situation where you should be reacting or relating differently? Describe.

Day 3 | *How Are You Wired?*

RESILIENCE

Let's begin with a definition of resilience and then we'll move into why it's important in your life.

Resilience is your ability to bounce back in the face of adversity and overcome the hurdles in your life. We believe it directly relates to your EQ—or Emotion Quotient—which measures your ability to understand your own emotions, to recognize the emotions of others, and to act appropriately based on this understanding.

It is also referred to as your Emotional Intelligence because it measures your aptitude for social and emotional interactions and skills that are critical for success in both a career and your relationships.

When compared to the more well-known Intelligence Quotient (IQ), there are two key differences between resilience and intelligence.

change your resilience

- First, more than 50 years of scientific research indicate that resilience may be more important for achieving success at work and satisfaction in life than IQ.
- Secondly, and perhaps even more importantly, you can change your resilience by changing your beliefs and the way you think.

By completing today's questionnaire, you will be objectively measuring your resilience in seven distinct categories:

1. Emotion Regulation
2. Impulse Control
3. Empathy
4. Optimism
5. Causal Analysis
6. Self-efficacy
7. Reaching Out

Tomorrow, you will score the results in each of these seven areas of resilience. You will learn how each category relates to the specific skills needed to cope effectively in life. Understanding and working to improve your resilience is critical for dealing with the unpredictable, and sometimes tragic, world in which we live. As we all know, it's not "if" life will include difficulties, but "what" they will be and "when" they will occur.

The good news is that resilience is under your control. It can be evaluated, learned, and modified. The authors of the book *The Resilience Factor*, Karen Reivich, Ph.D. and Andrew Shatté, Ph.D. say:

> "These skills are a means to achieve diverse ends—overcome childhood obstacles, steer through new adversities, bounce back from major setbacks, and reach out to broaden your world. In other words, they promote resilience, leading people to solve their own problems, take appropriate risks, and accurately forecast the implications of an adversity. These skills also provide a remarkable opportunity for people to look inward, to get to know themselves—really know themselves—and connect more deeply."

RESILIENCE QUESTIONNAIRE

Reivich and Shatté developed the following questionnaire and it has been incorporated into our program with their permission. It is the best assessment tool we have found for measuring and explaining the seven key elements of resilience. The first step in the process is to take an honest look at how you are doing in each of the seven categories; then you will be able to determine where additional work can be done to improve your skills.

Completing this assessment should only take about 10 minutes. Do not spend too much time on any one question. Your initial reaction is usually accurate. Please rate each item for how true it is of you, using the following scale:

1=not at all true
2=sometimes or somewhat true
3=moderately true
4=usually true
5=very true of me

______ 1. When trying to solve a problem, I trust my instincts and go with the first solution that occurs to me.

______ 2. Even if I plan ahead for a discussion with my boss, a coworker, my spouse, or my child, I still find myself acting emotionally.

______ 3. I worry about my future health.

______ 4. I am good at shutting out anything that distracts me from the task at hand.

______ 5. If my first solution doesn't work, I am able to go back and continue trying different solutions until I find one that works.

______ 6. I am curious.

______ 7. I am unable to harness positive emotions to help me to focus on a task.

_______ 8. I am the kind of person who likes to try new things.

_______ 9. I would rather do something at which I feel confident and relaxed than something that is quite challenging or difficult.

_______ 10. By looking at their facial expressions, I recognize the emotions people are experiencing.

_______ 11. I give in to the urge to give up when things go wrong.

_______ 12. When a problem arises, I come up with a lot of possible solutions before trying to solve it.

_______ 13. I can control the way I feel when adversity strikes.

_______ 14. What other people think about me does not influence my behavior.

_______ 15. When a problem occurs, I am aware of the first thoughts that pop into my head about it.

_______ 16. I feel most comfortable in situations in which I am not the only one responsible.

_______ 17. I prefer situations where I can depend on someone else's ability rather than my own.

_______ 18. I believe that it is better to believe that problems are always controllable, even if that is not always true.

_______ 19. When a problem arises, I think carefully about what caused it before attempting to solve it.

_______ 20. I have doubts about my ability to solve problems at work or at home.

_______ 21. I don't spend much time thinking about factors that are outside of my control.

_______ 22. I enjoy doing simple routine tasks that do not change.

_______ 23. I get carried away by my feelings.

_______ 24. It is difficult for me to understand why people feel the way they do.

_______ 25. I am good at identifying what I am thinking and how it affects my mood.

_______ 26. If someone does something that upsets me, I am able to wait until I have calmed down to discuss it.

_______ 27. When someone overreacts to a problem, I think that it is because they are in a bad mood that day.

_______ 28. I expect that I will do well on most things.

_______ 29. People often seek me out to help them figure out problems.

_______ 30. I feel at a loss to understand why people react as they do.

_______ 31. My emotions affect my ability to focus on what I need to get done at home, school, or at work.

_______ 32. Hard work always pays off.

_______ 33. After completing a task, I worry that it will be negatively evaluated.

_______ 34. If someone is sad, angry, or embarrassed, I have a good idea of what he or she may be thinking.

_______ 35. I don't like new challenges.

_______ 36. I don't plan ahead in my job, schoolwork, or finances.

_______ 37. If a colleague is upset, I have a pretty good idea why.

_______ 38. I prefer doing things spontaneously rather than planning ahead even if it means it doesn't turn out as well.

_______ 39. I believe that most problems are created by circumstances beyond my control.

_______ 40. I look at challenges as a way to learn and improve myself.

_______ 41. I've been told that I misinterpret events and situations.

_______ 42. If someone is upset with me, I listen to what they have to say before reacting.

_______ 43. When asked to think about my future, I find it hard to imagine myself as a success.

_______ 44. I've been told that I jump to conclusions when problems arise.

_______ 45. I am uncomfortable when meeting new people.

______ 46. It is easy for me to get "lost" in a book or a movie.

______ 47. I believe the old adage, "an ounce of prevention is worth a pound of cure."

______ 48. In most situations, I believe I'm good at identifying the true causes of problems.

______ 49. I believe that I have good coping skills and that I respond well to most challenges.

______ 50. My significant other and/or close friends tell me that I don't understand them.

______ 51. I am most comfortable in my established routines.

______ 52. I think it is important to solve problems as quickly as possible, even if that means sacrificing a full understanding of the problem.

______ 53. When faced with a difficult situation, I am confident that it will go well.

______ 54. My colleagues and friends tell me I don't listen to what they say.

______ 55. If I decide I want something, I go out and buy it right away.

______ 56. When I discuss a "hot" topic with a colleague or family member, I am able to keep my emotions in check.

WRAPPING IT UP

Warren Buffet, one of the wealthiest and most successful investment managers in the world, says, "Emotional stability trumps intellect."

Buffet goes on to say: "Emotional stability is more important than intellectual capability. No matter how bright you are, if you are not emotionally stable and confident in your abilities to do what you think is right, even when it's unpopular, you cannot achieve."

How true, yet the best words to describe resilience can be found in the Bible:

We are hard pressed on every side, but not crushed; perplexed but not in despair; persecuted but not abandoned; struck down but not destroyed. 2 Corinthians 4:8

The Lord is saying it is indeed possible to have faith that will not be shaken. You can be resilient and bounce back. You can even become better for having gone through the experience. In fact, it may be through these times that the Lord is equipping you to help others going through the same thing.

don't waste your pain

One of our basic assumptions: Don't waste your pain! It is through experiences requiring the greatest resilience that the Lord may be pointing you directly at the purpose He has for your life. Don't miss the message!

Describe a time when you relied on your emotional stability to get through a tough situation.

What do you think gave you the strength to remain stable in these circumstances? Explain.

Day 4 | How Are You Wired?

SCORING YOUR RESILIENCE QUESTIONNAIRE

The Resilience Questionnaire measures your level of proficiency in seven key areas. It provides a clear view of both your strengths and opportunities for improvement. Take your rating (1-5) for each question from yesterday's questionnaire and calculate your score as outlined below.

Instructions:
Score each of the seven areas of resilience, one at a time. Take a separate piece of paper and list the item numbers you need to score for each question. You can use that list of scores to post the applicable scores for each element of resilience. This will keep you from having to flip back and forth between the questionnaire and the score sheet.

1. Emotion Regulation

Post and add your scores on the following items:

Item 13	______	Item 2	______
Item 25	______	Item 7	______
Item 26	______	Item 23	______
Item 56	______	Item 31	______
Positive Total	______	Negative Total	______

Positive Total minus Negative Total = ______
This is your Emotional Regulation score.

Above Average:	A score higher than 13
Average:	A score between 6 and 13
Below Average:	A score lower than 6

control

what

you do

Emotion Regulation is the ability to stay calm under pressure. Resilient people use a well-developed set of skills that help them control their emotions, attention, and behavior. Strong emotion regulation means you can control the way you feel and what you do in the moment of adversity. It doesn't mean you don't have emotions. It simply means you have the ability to recognize intense emotions and handle them appropriately. Emotion Regulation is the most powerful of all the factors in resilience.

The Lord clearly tells us how to develop healthy skills that result in strong Emotion Regulation.

Do not be anxious about anything, but in everything, through prayer and petition, with thanksgiving, present your requests to the Lord. And the peace of God, which transcends all understanding will, guard your hearts and minds in Christ Jesus. Philippians 4:6-7

Being anxious encompasses strong emotions of worry, fear, and discontent—definitely not the peace of God we have been promised. But the Lord has an action plan: stop, pray, focus on being thankful, and then let Him guard your heart and mind when facing adversity.

It takes some practice but you can learn to do this. It helps you control your emotions and brings a sense of peace that goes far beyond what you could muster on your own!

2. Impulse Control

Post and add your scores on the following items:

Item 4	______	Item 11	______
Item 15	______	Item 36	______
Item 42	______	Item 38	______
Item 47	______	Item 55	______
Positive Total	______	Negative Total	______

Positive Total minus Negative Total = ______
This is your Impulse Control score.

Above Average:	A score higher than 0
Average:	A score between -6 and 0
Below Average:	A score lower than -6

Impulse control is the ability to delay gratification of desires. It means you can stop before you act. You can take the desire to do or say something you will probably regret and put it on hold. When you do act, it is with forethought and clarity—particularly as it relates to potential consequences.

Instead, clothe yourself with the presence of the Lord Jesus Christ. And don't let yourself think about ways to indulge your evil desires. Romans 13:14

If we do not learn to control our impulses and desires, we will (often without thinking) do things that are hurtful, harmful, and even sinful. Well-developed impulse control is an important part of learning to successfully deal with temptation in a sane, controlled, and positive way!

Watch and pray so that you will not fall into temptation. The Spirit is willing, but the body is weak. Matthew 26:41

The Two Big Ones

Impulse Control and Emotion Regulation are the two strongest factors determining your resilience quotient. The goal is to display emotions and behaviors that are productive and appropriate responses to the facts of the situation, not knee-jerk reactions that are raw and uncensored.

The Lord knows we will have emotions and impulses that should be managed and controlled. He knows we can be easily tempted to simply react rather than think. He tells us: ***In your anger, do not sin. Ephesians 4:26***

The Lord doesn't say do not get angry—He says do not sin. Anger, in and of itself, is not always a bad thing. In fact, it can be a valuable warning signal telling us something isn't quite right. What is important is how we decide to respond.

taking a realistic view

In our human nature, we will continually experience a whole host of desires, emotions, and impulses. But the most important question is: "What do we do with them?" Learning to stop, think, and formulate a wise, appropriate response is the key! It will undoubtedly lead to improved resilience and a life that honors the Lord and others!

3. Optimism

Post and add your scores on the following items:

Item 18	______	Item 3	______
Item 27	______	Item 33	______
Item 32	______	Item 39	______
Item 53	______	Item 43	______
Positive Total	______	Negative Total	______

Positive Total minus Negative Total = ______
This is your Optimism score.

Above Average:	A score higher than 6
Average:	A score between -2 and 6
Below Average:	A score lower than -2

Optimism means that you see your future as relatively bright. It is linked with self-efficacy and the belief that you can positively influence the world around you. Yet, the question that must be answered centers on realistic versus unrealistic optimism. It is not about putting your head in the sand and ignoring the problem, nor is it about simply giving up and assuming the worst. It is about taking a realistic view and staying hopeful as you work through the problems before you.

The key to optimism is challenging your beliefs and putting life events into a proper perspective. The Lord shows us the way when He says, ***Be joyful always; pray continually; give thanks in all circumstances. 1 Thessalonians 5:16***

Although this may seem to go against all your natural inclinations, the Lord is telling you that optimism is both possible and preferable. When you make the conscious decision to trust the Lord and realistically tackle your problems, you can learn to see people, circumstances and the future in a new, more positive light.

4. Causal Analysis

Post and add your scores on the following items:

Item 12	______	Item 1	______
Item 19	______	Item 41	______
Item 21	______	Item 44	______
Item 48	______	Item 52	______
Positive Total	______	Negative Total	______

Positive Total minus Negative Total = ______
This is your Causal Analysis score.

Above Average:	A score higher than 8
Average:	A score between 0 and 8
Below Average:	A score lower than 0

This is the ability to accurately identify the cause of your problems. Most resilient people are those who have the ability to identify the significant causes of the adversities they face. They are able to do this without falling into "all or nothing" extremes about the cause of their current situation. They are realists. They do not accept responsibility when it is not theirs to assume. They do not reflexively blame others and they do not ruminate about circumstances outside their control.

As with all the elements of resilience, the Lord gives insight on how to improve our causal analysis. One example is in Psalm 139:23 where He shows us what it looks like to take a realistic and honest view of ourselves. In this poignant excerpt, David cries out to the Lord:

Search me, O God, and know my heart; test me and know my anxious thoughts. See if there is any offensive way in me, and lead me in the way everlasting.

Now that's a brave prayer! But we all need to know the truth about ourselves if we hope to be skilled in this area of causal analysis.

For those who struggle with causal analysis, it is typically grounded in the inability to see where personal responsibility begins and ends. It also indicates an inability to see the role others are playing in the situation. If you find you're having trouble "connecting the dots" between cause and result, it is time to courageously seek the Lord by praying this Psalm. Allow the Lord to give you wisdom, enlightenment, and a greater ability to assess and respond appropriately.

5. Empathy

Post and add your scores on the following items:

Item 10	______	Item 24	______
Item 34	______	Item 30	______
Item 37	______	Item 50	______
Item 46	______	Item 54	______
Positive Total	______	Negative Total	______

Positive Total minus Negative Total = ______
This is your Empathy score.

Above Average:	A score higher than 12
Average:	A score between 3 and 12
Below Average:	A score lower than 3

Your empathy score represents how well you are able to read the cues other people present about their psychological and emotional states. It also measures your ability to respond to those cues by assessing how well you can identify with the feelings, thoughts, or attitudes of others. Being sensitive to others promotes better communication, understanding, and cooperation. On a deeper level, it reflects your ability to "feel for others" and show a caring attitude toward things they care about.

Administer true justice; show mercy and compassion to one another. Do not oppress the widow or the fatherless, the alien or the poor. In your hearts do not think evil of each other. Zechariah 7:9-10

have faith in your ability to succeed

Mercy may not be your gift, and you may find it difficult to understand and show empathy when you have not walked in the shoes of the other person. But sensitivity can be learned and cultivated. Training your heart and mind through Scripture is a powerful way to learn what the Lord would have you do. Use the concordance in your Bible or visit www.biblegateway.com. Search for the keywords mercy, love, and compassion to find verses that can guide you in developing greater empathy.

6. Self-Efficacy

Post and add your scores on the following items:

Item 5	______	Item 9	______
Item 28	______	Item 17	______
Item 29	______	Item 20	______
Item 49	______	Item 22	______
Positive Total	______	Negative Total	______

Positive Total minus Negative Total = ______
This is your Self-efficacy score.

Above Average:	A score higher than 10
Average:	A score between 6 and 10
Below Average:	A score lower than 6

This relates to the sense that you are effective in the world. It is the belief that you can solve problems that you face and have faith in your ability to succeed. People with high self-efficacy scores often emerge as leaders because they can see possibilities and alternatives that allow them to overcome obstacles and be victorious in their pursuits. Those with strong self-efficacy also demonstrate a robust ability to literally "throw off" hindrances, hang tough in the face of adversity, and persevere with strength and stamina.

Throw off everything that hinders...and run with perseverance the race set out before you. Hebrews 12:1

Self-efficacy can be developed and improved when you identify the blocks and limiting beliefs standing in your way. In Step 4 of this program, we will be working with you to identify those roadblocks and help you address them. This will greatly enhance your ability to move forward with confidence, tackle problems head-on, and believe in your ability to succeed.

7. Reaching Out

Post and add your scores on the following items:

Item 6	______	Item 16	______
Item 8	______	Item 35	______
Item 14	______	Item 45	______
Item 40	______	Item 51	______
Positive Total	______	Negative Total	______

Positive Total minus Negative Total = ______
This is your Reaching Out score.

step out unafraid

Above Average:	A score higher than 9
Average:	A score between 4 and 9
Below Average:	A score lower than 4

Reaching out measures how comfortable you are at taking risks in different areas of your life. A surprising number of people fear reaching out. For some, it is the fear of embarrassment, ridicule, or public failure. They think it is better to risk a life of mediocrity than to be exposed to such adversity. It can also reflect an overall fear of failure that says "it is better not to try than to end up failing."

Reaching out is definitely a learned skill. You may be inhibited from reaching out because of past experiences that have hurt or frightened you. But through this program we will help you see your past experiences, your gifts, skills, and talents as uniquely crafted and given by the Lord. In Step 4, we will also deal directly with any fears that might stop you from being all that God has planned. We will help you prepare to step out unafraid in the purpose He has for you!

The Lord knows that fear is a strong emotion. Left unaddressed, it can paralyze you and prevent you from being and doing all that He desires. Our goal is to help you identify your fears, bring them out in the light, and smooth a pathway through them toward your purpose. We look forward to helping you say,

I sought the Lord and he answered me, He delivered me from all my fears. Psalm 34:4

WRAPPING IT UP

Wow! We've covered a lot of ground today. Hopefully you've found this part of your journey both informative and thought-provoking.

Tomorrow we will conclude our look at resilience and talk more about how the Lord can provide tools to help you improve your skills in the areas where you didn't score as well as you might have liked.

Remember: there is no pass or fail. This is all about new self-awareness, acceptance, and a chance to make positive changes in your life.

Conclude today by journaling thoughts and feelings about what you have just learned.

Day 5 | *How Are You Wired?*

A DEEPER LOOK AT RESILIENCE

As you look back over your scores from yesterday's resiliency assessment, remember that research has powerfully demonstrated resilience to be one of the most significant keys to success in life. It is your "thinking style" and beliefs that determine your level of resilience. It is the lens through which you view the world.

Based on yesterday's results, list the areas where you had the highest scores:

List the areas where you had the lowest scores:

How important are each of these areas in your life and why?

According to Reivich and Shatté, there are four fundamental uses for resilience:

1. **Overcome** the obstacles of your childhood and your past: broken home, poverty, neglect, abandonment, bullying, abuse.
2. **Steer through** the everyday adversities that befall you, i.e. arguments, disagreements, stress, and hassles.
3. **Bounce back** from traumatic events or difficulties rather than becoming helpless and resigned.
4. **Reach out** as a proactive means of connecting with others, pursuing new activities, and becoming strong and courageous in all you undertake.

Gaining resilience will help with all four of these uses. Which is the area you could benefit from the most? Why?

ANSWERS IN GOD'S WORD

While your DISC or primary personality style almost always remains the same throughout your life, you can change your Resilience Quotient by consciously addressing areas where you may be falling short. In fact, we believe the easiest way to improve your resilience can be found in your relationship with the Lord and the teachings of the Bible.

We're not aware of any formal studies that show a definitive correlation between people who have a mature relationship with the Lord and higher scores on the Resilience Questionnaire, but we have seen significant differences as we work through **7 Steps to Purpose** with our clients.

the Lord can transform

People who trust in the Word of the Lord, regularly study the Scriptures, and have a mature, trusting relationship with the Lord, are far more resilient! They are better able to see the joy and abundance in their lives even when bad things happen. They are able to concentrate on their blessings instead of their obstacles. They know they can have a positive impact on the world around them yet have a deep dependence on the Lord and His power in their lives.

Knowing this connection, you will recall that we tied Scripture to each of the seven elements as you scored your Resilience Questionnaire. We did this to demonstrate the close correlation between the two. We believe:

- Studying and internalizing Scripture directly impacts your values and beliefs.
- Your values and beliefs directly impact your resilience.
- Your resilience is critically important for achieving success in life.

When it comes to God's role in shaping your beliefs—and therefore your level of resilience—consider this Scripture:

Don't copy the behavior and customs of this world, but let God transform you into a new person by changing the way you think. Romans 12:2 (NLT)

The Lord can transform your mind and thus your beliefs. But, time getting to know God is required. The best way to do that is to spend time reading the Bible. We have heard it said many ways, but the Bible is the Lord's Word. It is His voice to humanity. It is not just a collection of good stories or a heavy-handed rule book. It is wisdom and guidance for everyday living. It tells of the trustworthiness of the Lord's character and His deep and abiding love and forgiveness. It is His "love letter" to mankind.

As you allow your beliefs to become more closely aligned with the Lord's goodness and His promises, the more resilient you will become. It's not about being a "Pollyanna" and ignoring reality. It's about believing you can—with the Lord's help—stand strong, persevere, and make it through your difficulties. It's learning where to put your focus: Not on your problem, but on the presence and strength that only the Lord can provide.

Here is an important thought to bear in mind as you focus on improving your resilience:

Trust in the LORD with all your heart and lean not on your own understanding; in all your ways acknowledge him, and he will make your paths straight. Proverbs 3:5-6

DIVE DEEPER

Learn more about developing the foundational skills you need to overcome areas of weakness and enhance areas of strength by reading *The Resilience Factor: 7 Essential Skills for Overcoming Life's Inevitable Obstacles* by Karen Reivich, Ph.D., and Andrew Shatté, Ph.D. You can find this book at www.IdentityandDestiny.com in our Recommended Reading Section, linked directly to Amazon for easy purchase.

Another valuable resource is available through the Hay Group. *The Resilience Workbook- Managing Change, Facing Adversity and Bouncing Back* is a 30 page workbook that provides all the basic principles on Resilience in a very understandable fashion. It can be purchased at www.haygroup.com or link directly to the purchase location by going to http://bit.ly/dTiaew.

Earlier today we said, "Your beliefs directly impact your resilience." Where do your beliefs come from?

When placed in that context, how much can you rely upon your current belief system?

Not real sure how to answer these questions? We'll be talking more about beliefs as we move into Step 2 and identify your core values. Every step in the process is part of gathering the pieces of your mosaic. In the end, they all fit together and one step leads to the next.

You do the steps—God does the rest!

WRAPPING IT UP

Take time now to think about why it might be important for you to work on improving areas of resilience that were not as strong as you would like them to be. List the areas you would like to improve.

Search your Bible, go to www.biblegateway.com, or ask a trusted spiritual leader or friend to identify Scripture that will help you make the changes you desire. List them below and make a point of reading them regularly. Let the Lord's Word renew and transform your mind.

IDENTITY AND DESTINY COACHES AVAILABLE!

While we've designed the **7 Steps** workbook to be completely sufficient as a self-guided study for both small groups and individuals, this is one of those places where having a trained coach can help optimize your experience. We encourage you to visit www.IdentityandDestiny.com and learn more about the coaches who have completed our certified training programs and the "laser coaching" sessions we've created to target specific concerns without requiring a long-term commitment. Custom-designed services provide the help, support, and encouragement you need. All inquiries are strictly confidential. (Coaches are available by telephone or Skype so geographic location is not an issue.)

PLEASE NOTE: If you would like to learn more about becoming an *Identity and Destiny* Certified Program Leader, please contact us at www.IdentityandDestiny.com.

Review | *How Are You Wired?*

KEY POINTS TO REMEMBER!

- Your primary DISC personality style shows the basic motivation that drives your behavior, your best situations and environments, and your best way of communicating, interacting with others, and making decisions.
- There is no right or wrong. Embrace who you are, love how you are wired, and run with it!
- The Lord has a plan for your life and He has wired you perfectly for that purpose. The goal is self-awareness and acceptance.
- Resilience is your ability to bounce back in the face of adversity and overcome obstacles. Research continues to show it is critical to success in life. The good news is it can be learned, modified, and improved.
- The Lord can transform your mind and thus your beliefs, but it requires that you invest time getting to know Him. The best way to do that is consistently reading the Bible!
- Studying and internalizing Scripture will directly, and positively, impact your values, beliefs, and resilience.

My Big "Aha"
List the most dramatic or important things you discovered or learned this week.

Capture It!
Go back through this weeks work and record the words, phrases, pictures, feelings, concepts, and key thoughts that have come from this week's work.

God's Word
Identify the Scripture that impacted you most deeply this week and journal your thoughts in this format:

Write out the Scripture:

Identify it's **Message** to you.

How can you **Apply** it to your life?

Write a **Prayer** back to the Lord about this Scripture. Thank Him, ask for help, or just talk about it with Him, whatever feels right.

Personal Notes, Thoughts, and Journaling

STEP 2 | WEEK THREE

What Makes You Tick?

TOP 5 CORE VALUES

DOMINANT SPIRITUAL GIFT

Day 1 | What Makes You Tick?

CORE VALUES AND WHY THEY MATTER

Core values are not just preferences or priorities; they are born out of your most deeply held beliefs. They point to what's genuinely important to you and shape—at the deepest level—your behavior, choices, and decisions.

Core values are also a critical part of your purpose. We like to call them "guardrails on the highway of life." They're a big part of answering the question: "Who am I?"

living in opposition to your core values in down right exhausting

If you haven't clearly defined your values, you'll often feel like you're simply drifting along in life. Instead of basing your decisions on a well-defined internal compass, you'll end up making choices based on emotion, circumstances, and social pressure as you try to fulfill other people's expectations instead of your own. You end up living like ***A wave of the sea, blown and tossed by the wind…double-minded and unstable. James 1: 7- 8***

Trying to be someone else and living without—or in opposition to—your core values is downright exhausting. It leaves you feeling empty, frustrated, and confused. Conversely, living life in line with your core values brings certainty, direction, and peace. Who couldn't use a little more of that?

WHERE ARE YOU NOW?

The first three days of this week will be devoted to identifying and confirming your most important core values. We will also help you analyze how well your life actually reflects those values. But, before we begin, let's take a look at where you are now:

Can you list three or four core values you believe guide your life today?

Do you know where these core values come from?

Do you feel like your daily life reflects the importance of these core values? Briefly explain.

VALUES CAN CHANGE YOUR LIFE FOR THE BETTER!

We all have values that guide our lives, but the important question is: Are you consciously aware of them?

Your values and beliefs have been developed and internalized based on life experience. They impact you each and every day. We will not only help you become consciously aware of your core values but determine whether there are changes you want to make.

Remember: When well-chosen core values guide your life you eliminate the internal strife that comes from living in opposition to what's truly important.

Living without clearly defined core values is like steering a ship without a rudder: no direction, no control, no guidance system.

Living in opposition to your core values is like sailing a boat against the wind: struggle, frustration, little forward momentum.

But living according to your core values means smooth sailing ahead.

FILTERS AND PRISMS

With these thoughts in mind, let us share some insight from the book titled *Teach Yourself NLP* (Neuro-linguistic Programming) by Steve Bavister and Amanda Vickers:

- Beliefs, and in particular, values, are important because they are the filters through which we see the world around us. They reflect generalizations we have made about the world and they motivate us to choose certain paths and plans for our lives. We tend to move toward what we value and away from what we don't.
- Most importantly, values provide maximum leverage for change in your life. Let us explain. If you only change your environment, behavior, or capabilities, the transformation may be short-lived. However, if you choose to change your values and beliefs, you are then working at the level of your identity and spirituality.

values

provide

leverage

According to Bavister and Vickers, values and beliefs are the most powerful area for leveraging change in your life! As you work through the **7 Steps to Purpose,** that is exactly what you will be doing.

The good news is that values are not innate. They are developed over your lifetime and they can be changed and adapted. When we get to Step 4 of this program, we will focus specifically on blocks and limiting beliefs. This is an extension of values and beliefs, but they are ones that are not working well for you. Still, they have somehow become the prism through which you view the world. We will help you identify those that may be roadblocks to your purpose. We will show you how to smooth a path through them and make positive, long-term change in your life.

Can you list any values or beliefs that might be limiting you?

Where did those values and beliefs come from?

What impact have they had on your life?

"SHOULD" VERSUS "CHOSEN" VALUES

One more understanding that is going to be important to this week's work is the concept of "should" versus "chosen" values. The core values we will be seeking in this week's exercise are those that are consciously chosen. They're incorporated into the fabric of who you are because they truly matter.

We are not looking for your "should" values. These are usually lifestyle-based, reactionary values that are influenced by:

- pride and ego
- pressure from the world around you
- expectations of others.

The three big drivers in our society for these superficial kinds of values are power, prestige, and image. They usually boil down to what you think others want from you and generally do not reflect your true core values. The important thing as you do tomorrow's exercise is to really listen with your heart. You want to choose the values that resonate deep from within.

WRAPPING IT UP

Can you think of a time when a lack of certainty made you feel like "a wave of the sea, blown and tossed by the wind"? Explain.

Do you think a lack of clearly defined core values contributed to this situation? Explain.

Looking back, did conflict between "should" versus "chosen" values have anything to do with your uncertainty?

In retrospect, what values would you choose to guide your choices or decisions in that same circumstance?

Day 2 | *What Makes You Tick?*

IDENTIFYING YOUR CORE VALUES

listen with your heart

Today we are going to go through a process that will allow you to identify your top five core values. Remembering yesterday's discussion regarding "should" versus "chosen" values, we want you to think of your chosen values as you complete today's exercise. Focus on those values that are most important to you, not those that should be important. Think about each word—and listen with your heart!

ESTABLISHING CORE VALUES

Instructions:

Go through all 80 words in column 1, comparing two words at a time. For example, compare words 1 and 2, pick the word that is most important to you, and enter it in column 2. Compare words 3 and 4, pick the word that is most important to you, and enter it in the next space in column 2. When you have done this for all 80 words in column 1 then do the same for the 40 words remaining in column 2.

At the point that you have 20 words in column 3, take a look at that list and see how it "feels" to you. Then take each of the 20 words and follow the branch back through columns 1 and 2 to see if there are words that resonate strongly but may have missed the cut or appear to be duplicated by other words. If you want to make changes to this list based on your review, feel free to do so before you move forward.

Next, resume the comparison and process of elimination for the 20 words remaining in column 3. This will then result in the top 10 words (or core values) remaining in column 4.

As you work through the assessment, journal notes about your thoughts and feelings. Were you challenged with specific decisions? Values really matter and can evoke strong reactions. Record those reactions as they occur.

Column 1	Column 2	Column 3	Column 4
1. Acceptance	(1)	-1-	{1}
2. Accountability			
3. Achievement	(2)		
4. Attitude			
5. Authenticity	(3)	-2-	
6. Balance			
7. Boldness	(4)		
8. Character			
9. Collaboration	(5)	-3-	{2}
10. Commitment			
11. Compassion	(6)		
12. Competence			
13. Confidence	(7)	-4-	
14. Contentment			
15. Courage	(8)		
16. Creativity			
17. Dedication	(9)	-5-	{3}
18. Dependability			
19. Devotion	(10)		
20. Discipline			
21. Discovery	(11)	-6-	
22. Diversity			
23. Efficiency	(12)		
24. Empathy			
25. Encouragement	(13)	-7-	{4}
26. Endurance			
27. Enthusiasm	(14)		
28. Excellence			
29. Fairness	(15)	-8-	
30. Family			
31. Fitness	(16)		
32. Generosity			

Value	Pair	Group	Set
33. Gentleness	(17)	-9-	{5}
34. Goodness			
35. Growth	(18)		
36. Honesty			
37. Honor	(19)	-10	
38. Hope			
39. Humility	(20)		
40. Humor			
41. Independence	(21)	-11-	{6}
42. Integrity			
43. Intimacy	(22)		
44. Joy			
45. Justice	(23)	-12-	
46. Kindness			
47. Leadership	(24)		
48. Learning			
49. Love	(25)	-13-	{7}
50. Loyalty			
51. Obedience	(26)		
52. Openness			
53. Order	(27)	-14-	
54. Passion			
55. Patience	(28)		
56. Peace			
57. Perseverance	(29)	-15-	{8}
58. Personal Growth			
59. Quality	(30)		
60. Relationships			
61. Reliability	(31)	-16-	
62. Respect			
63. Sacrifice	(32)		
64. Security			

65. Self-control	(33)	-17-	{9}
66. Self-discipline			
67. Selflessness	(34)		
68. Simplicity			
69. Spirituality	(35)	-18-	
70. Steadfast			
71. Submission	(36)		
72. Teachable			
73. Teamwork	(37)	-19-	{10}
74. Thankfulness			
75. Tranquility	(38)		
76. Transparency			
77. Trustworthiness	(39)	-20-	
78. Truth			
79. Unity	(40)		
80. Wisdom			

WRAPPING IT UP

From the 10 core values in Column 4, pick your top five.

1.	2.	3.	4.	5.

Some people can establish a single dominant core value, others have a problem selecting between the five top values they have chosen. Can you pick a top core value?

your internal compass

Were there any values that did not make the top five that you feel very strongly about? Make a note of them along with your list of five above. It's okay to keep them on your list but remember that the point is to identify and know what you value most. Then you can truly establish a value system that can be used as an internal compass guiding your thoughts, actions, and choices.

When it all came together, were there any surprises in your top five core values? Why?

In evaluating your core values, where do you think they came from?

Tomorrow we'll take a look at how well you live up to your top values. How do you think you'll score there and why?

First Corinthians 13 is the Bible's "love chapter." In the first verse the Lord says, ***And now I will show you the most excellent way.***

He concludes the chapter saying, ***And now these three remain: faith, hope and love. But the greatest of these is love.***

Regardless of the values you choose and the gifts you possess, the Lord says love must be at the heart of them all!

Day 3 | What Makes You Tick?

ARE YOU LIVING ACCORDING TO YOUR CORE VALUES?

Now that you have identified your top five core values, you may find yourself thinking there is still a measurable difference between the "you that you want to be" and the "you that you are." This may not be a comfortable thought but it's important to acknowledge. It can be a red-flag indicator of conflict that has the potential to produce high levels of internal stress. The good news is that it is all part of the process. The first step toward reducing this kind of stress and living according to your chosen core values is knowing what they are. Then you can work to clearly articulate them and begin to make choices and decisions in line with those values.

This next exercise allows you to take a look at how well you're currently incorporating your core values into your daily life. Living within those values is critical to your personal satisfaction and comfort. If you're making choices based on your core values, it will help erase an enormous amount of conflict and bring a new level of peace into your life.

ARE YOU LIVING YOUR CORE VALUES?

At the beginning of each of the five scoring charts below, write down one of the top five core values identified in yesterday's exercise. Then, circle the number that correlates with how well you are incorporating that value into each area of your life.

Please feel free to make notes in the margin as you think about the importance of each core value as it relates to that area of your life.

Core Value 1: ___________________________

1-not often 2-occasionally 3-regularly 4-always

Family	1	2	3	4
Work	1	2	3	4
Spiritual life	1	2	3	4
Finances	1	2	3	4
Friends/leisure	1	2	3	4

Total score for this value: ___________

Core Value 2: ___________________________

1-not often 2-occasionally 3-regularly 4-always

Family	1	2	3	4
Work	1	2	3	4
Spiritual life	1	2	3	4
Finances	1	2	3	4
Friends/leisure	1	2	3	4

Total score for this value: _______________

Core Value 3: ___________________________

1-not often 2-occasionally 3-regularly 4-always

Family	1	2	3	4
Work	1	2	3	4
Spiritual life	1	2	3	4
Finances	1	2	3	4
Friends/leisure	1	2	3	4

Total score for this value: ____________

Core Value 4: ___________________________

1-not often 2-occasionally 3-regularly 4-always

Family	1	2	3	4
Work	1	2	3	4
Spiritual life	1	2	3	4
Finances	1	2	3	4
Friends/leisure	1	2	3	4

Total score for this value: ______________

Core Value 5: ________________________

1-not often 2-occasionally 3-regularly 4-always

Family	1	2	3	4
Work	1	2	3	4
Spiritual life	1	2	3	4
Finances	1	2	3	4
Friends/leisure	1	2	3	4

Total score for this value: ____________

LIVING YOUR CORE VALUES/SCORING ANALYSIS: PART 1

Each core value has a possible score of 20.
Write the value and score for each of your five core values in the boxes below:

1.	2.	3.	4.	5.

Review each core value according to the scoring category that applies:

15 to 20: You're on target! You're doing an excellent job of living your core values and thus minimizing the internal stress in your life. In all likelihood, you have previously made a concerted effort to know your core values and use them as a guide for your life and the choices you make. Remember to stay focused on your core values and continue using them as your guide. A values-based life doesn't happen by accident. It is a choice, a conscious act of the will.

10 to 15: You're able to incorporate core values into most of your day-to-day life, but there's room for improvement. Take a look at the areas where you scored the lowest and see if you can consciously change how you live those values. For instance, if a core value is "excellence," but you consistently bounce checks and incur overdraft fees in your financial life, you're not living in harmony with your core values.

Less than 10: Experience shows that you're living with serious internal stress as a result of making decisions based on core values less than half of the time. Take a long and serious look at each of those points and determine what you can do to make a difference. Look for the low-hanging fruit so you can feel the change quickly. For instance, if a core value is "discovery," but you go for days without learning new things, schedule time for discovery. That might be as easy as downloading books or podcasts and then listening to them on your commute or as you exercise. Recognize that living according to your core values will pay enormous returns in your health and satisfaction in life.

LIVING YOUR CORE VALUES/SCORING ANALYSIS: PART 2

Each area of your life also has a possible score of 20.
Total your score for each of the five areas of life and post below:

1. Family	2. Work	3. Spiritual	4. Finances	5. Friends

Based on the lowest scores directly above, are there particular areas of your life that seem to be getting "the short end of the stick" when it comes to living according to your core values?

What obstacles are standing in your way? Is it a matter of priorities? Is it a lack of clarity that can now be seen and corrected?

Balance is a choice and takes concerted effort and discipline. With the Lord's help, you can make changes that will enhance every area of your life. What action steps can you take now to begin integrating your core values into every area of life?

There is a time for everything, and a season for every activity under heaven. Ecclesiastes 3:1

LIVING YOUR VALUES

If you're living a "values-based" life, you are:

- certain of the values that guide your life,
- able to determine what choices, events, and people align with those values, and
- willing to make decisions based on your values.

On the other hand, far too many people live what we call a "desires-based" life. Without knowing your values and purpose, you have:

- no moral compass and look to others for validation and direction,
- soft boundaries and lack certainty, and
- difficulty staying true to your own values and beliefs.

change your values

Remember: you can change your values! But it first takes self-awareness and a conscious decision to make the change. It also requires a trustworthy source as your guide. As you might suspect, we recommend prayer and Scripture:

Your word is a lamp to my feet and a light for my path. Psalm 119:105

Seeking the Lord's wisdom, clearly identifying your core values, and making a commitment to live by them is an important part of being able to live as God describes:

Do not conform any longer to the patterns of this world, but be transformed by the renewing of your mind. Then you will be able to test and approve the will of God for your life, His good, pleasing and perfect will. Romans 12:2

Your core values should guide your life. Live by them and you will find peace and satisfaction. Ignore them and you'll find yourself feeling miserable. You may not know why you're feeling internal conflict and stress until you take the time to really look at your core values, where they come from, and why you consider them important.

But know this: your values have a direct impact on how you feel, how you behave, and how you make choices.

Choose wisely!

WRAPPING IT UP

Based on the work you've done the past two days:

From memory, list your top five core values.

Now that you've had a couple of days to think about it, can you identify your top core value?

Reflect on a typical week in your life. Are you using your time, talent, and financial resources in a way that reflects your core values as your true priority? Can you list some examples?

What are three positive changes you will commit to making that can help you live a values-based life and gain greater balance in all areas of your life?

What results are you hoping to achieve with these changes?

Trust in the LORD with all your heart and lean not on your own understanding; in all your ways acknowledge him, and he will make your paths straight. Proverbs 3: 5-6

Day 4 | What Makes You Tick?

DISCOVERING YOUR DOMINANT SPIRITUAL GIFT

Spiritual gifts come directly from the Lord and are an important part of how you've been uniquely gifted to accomplish your God-given purpose.

fruitfulness

not

weariness

Just as each of us has one body with many members, and these members do not all have the same function, so in Christ we who are many form one body, and each member belongs to all the others. We have different gifts, according to the grace given us. Romans 12:4-6

Bill Gothard is founder of the Institute of Basic Life Principles (IBLP) and has studied spiritual gifts extensively. He writes: "Knowing that we each have a gift that is valuable to the Body of Christ, we are able to achieve a deeper level of self-acceptance and purpose in life."

Boy, does that line up with the work you are doing in the **7 Steps to Purpose**!

Gothard goes on to say, "As we exercise our gifts, we experience personal fulfillment and a deep sense of joy. By concentrating on our gifts, we achieve maximum fruitfulness with minimum weariness."

Doesn't that sound like a great way to live?

IDENTIFYING YOUR SPIRITUAL GIFTS

The following exercises are based upon Gothard's work and we gratefully thank him and IBLP (www.iblp.org) for their generous consent to incorporate this spiritual gifts inventory into our workbook.

You'll complete four exercises today then one more tomorrow to pinpoint what Gothard calls your motivational gift. We will be referring to it in our writing as your dominant spiritual gift.

SPIRITUAL GIFTS INVENTORY: EXERCISE 1

Seven People: Which One Is YOU?
This exercise is designed to help you objectively search for your dominant spiritual gift by asking you to score various statements based on your level of agreement.

Rate your answers with the number that best describes you in relation to *each and every statement* listed for each of the seven people. Place your answer in the box beside each question then average your score for each section as noted.

You must score every statement for every person.

0 = Never 1 = Occasionally 2 = Often 3 = Always

PERSON 1

1. You want to make sure that statements are true and accurate. ______
2. You desire to gain as much knowledge as you can. ______
3. You react to people who make unfounded statements. ______
4. You check the credentials of one who wants to teach you. ______
5. You use your mind to check out an argument. ______
6. You enjoy spending hours doing research on a subject. ______
7. You like to tell others as many facts as you can on a topic. ______
8. You pay close attention to words and phrases. ______
9. You tend to be silent on a matter until you check it out. ______
10. You like to study material in a systematic sequence. ______

Total Points for Person 1 _______
AVERAGE FOR PERSON 1—Divide total by 10 _______

PERSON 2

1. You can visualize the final result of a major undertaking. ______
2. You enjoy coordinating the efforts of many to reach a common goal. ______
3. You can break down a large task into achievable goals. ______
4. You are able to delegate assignments to others. ______
5. You see people as resources that can be used to get a job done. ______
6. You are willing to endure difficulties to accomplish a task. ______
7. You require loyalty from those who are under your supervision. ______
8. You remove yourself from petty details to focus on the final goal. ______
9. You can encourage your workers and inspire them to action. ______
10. You move on to a new challenge once a job is finished. ______

Total Points for Person 2 ________
AVERAGE FOR PERSON 2—Divide total by 10 ________

PERSON 3

1. You see actions as either right or wrong. ______
2. You react strongly to people who are not what they appear to be. ______
3. You can quickly detect when something is not what it appears to be. ______
4. You can quickly discern a person's character. ______
5. You feel a responsibility to correct those who do wrong. ______
6. You separate yourself from those who refuse to repent of evil. ______
7. You explain what is wrong with an item before you sell it. ______
8. You let people know how you feel about important issues. ______
9. You enjoy people who are completely honest with you. ______
10. You are quick to judge yourself when you fail. ______
11. You are willing to do the right thing even if it means suffering alone for it. ______

Total Points for Person 3 ________
AVERAGE FOR PERSON 3—Divide total by 11 ________

PERSON 4

1. You can sense when people have hurt feelings. ______
2. You react to people who are insensitive to other's feelings. ______
3. You are able to discern genuine love. ______
4. You desire deep friendships in which there is mutual commitment. ______
5. You seem to attract people who tell you their problems. ______
6. You find it difficult to be firm or decisive with people. ______
7. You tend to take up offenses for those whom you love. ______
8. You need quality time to explain how you feel. ______
9. You want to remove those who cause hurt to others. ______
10. You often wonder why God allows people to suffer. ______

Total Points for Person 4 _________
AVERAGE FOR PERSON 4—Divide total by 10 _________

PERSON 5

1. You motivate people to become what you see they could be. ______
2. You like to give counsel in logical steps of action. ______
3. You can usually discern a person's level of spiritual maturity. ______
4. You enjoy working out projects to help people grow spiritually. ______
5. You sometimes raise expectations of results prematurely. ______
6. You dislike teaching that does not give practical direction. ______
7. You like to see the facial responses of those whom you counsel. ______
8. You often take "family time" to counsel others. ______
9. You enjoy giving examples from the lives of others. ______
10. You soon give up on those who do not follow your counsel. ______
11. You find it hard to follow through on the project you have started. ______
12. You identify with people where they are in order to counsel them. ______

Total Points for Person 5 _________
AVERAGE FOR PERSON 5—Divide total by 12 _________

PERSON 6

1. You notice the practical needs of others and enjoy meeting them. ______
2. You enjoy serving to free others for more important things. ______
3. You are willing to neglect your own work to help others. ______
4. You sometimes go beyond your physical strength to help others. ______
5. You can remember the likes and dislikes of others. ______
6. You can usually detect ways to serve before anyone else can. ______
7. You will be prepared to use your own funds to get a job done quickly. ______
8. You do not mind doing jobs by yourself. ______
9. You do not want public praise but you do need to feel appreciated. ______
10. You find it difficult to say "no" to those who ask for help. ______
11. You like to put "extra touches" on the jobs that you do. ______

Total Points for Person 6 ________
AVERAGE FOR PERSON 6—Divide total by 11 ________

PERSON 7

1. You are frugal with money for yourself and your family. ______
2. You enjoy investing money in the ministries of other people. ______
3. You have an ability to make money by wise investments. ______
4. You desire to keep your giving a secret. ______
5. You react negatively to pressure appeals for money. ______
6. You like to encourage others to give with your gifts. ______
7. You want ministries you support to be as effective as possible. ______
8. You enjoy giving to needs that others often overlook. ______
9. You sometimes fear your gifts will corrupt those who get them. ______
10. You desire to give gifts of high quality. ______
11. You enjoy knowing that your gifts were specific answers to prayer. ______

Total Points for Person 7 ________
AVERAGE FOR PERSON 7—Divide total by 11 ________

Take a look at your average score for each person. Which person did you score the highest average for? Circle your answer below:

Person 1: TEACHER
Person 2: ORGANIZER
Person 3: PROPHET
Person 4: MERCY
Person 5: EXHORTER
Person 6: SERVER
Person 7: GIVER

SPIRITUAL GIFTS INVENTORY: EXERCISE 2

People and Irritations: Another Way to Find Your Gift
This exercise is designed to use "irritations" from others as another part of discovering your dominant spiritual gift. When something really bothers you, it may be that it flies in the face of how you are spiritually wired. Your answers to the following questions will be greatly influenced by your spiritual gift.

Begin by answering these two questions:

1. What one thing irritates you most in other Christians? Explain.

2. What one thing irritates you most in other people? Explain.

There are seven possible responses listed below. Put a check in the box next to the one single reaction that most closely resembles your answers to the above questions.

1. They compromise with the world. ❒
2. They fail to demonstrate true Christian concern. ❒
3. They are substituting experience for sound doctrine. ❒
4. They are not growing to spiritual maturity. ❒
5. They are not trusting God for their finances. ❒
6. They are not accomplishing any major goals. ❒
7. They do not have genuine love for each other. ❒

Circle Your Answer Below:

If you checked 1: PROPHET
If you checked 2: SERVER
If you checked 3: TEACHER
If you checked 4: EXHORTER
If you checked 5: GIVER
If you checked 6: ORGANIZER
If you checked 7: MERCY

SPIRITUAL GIFTS INVENTORY: EXERCISE 3

What Basic Motivation Says About Your Dominant Spiritual Gift
A family of seven is gathered for Sunday lunch and each family member possesses one of the seven motivational gifts. When someone drops the dessert tray onto the floor, here is what each might say. Which one most closely represents what you would say?

1. "That's what happens when you're not careful!"
   (Motivation: To correct the problem.) ❐

2. "Oh! Let me help you clean it up."
   (Motivation: To fulfill an intangible need.) ❐

3. "The reason it fell is because it was too heavy on one side."
   (Motivation: To discover why it happened.) ❐

4. "Next time, let's serve the dessert with the meal."
   (Motivation: To correct the future.) ❐

5. "I'll be happy to buy a new dessert."
   (Motivation: To meet a tangible need.) ❐

6. "Jim, would you get the mop. Sue, please help pick it up; and Mary, help me fix another dessert."
   (Motivation: To achieve the immediate goal of the group.) ❐

7. "Don't feel badly, it could have happened to anyone."
   (Motivation: To correct the problem.) ❐

Circle Your Answer Below:

Member 1: PROPHET
Member 2: SERVER
Member 3: TEACHER
Member 4: EXHORTER
Member 5: GIVER
Member 6: ORGANIZER
Member 7: MERCY

SPIRITUAL GIFTS INVENTORY: EXERCISE 4

Understanding How Each Gift Responds in a Situation
Seven Christians paid a visit to a sick person in the hospital, each representing one of the motivational gifts. Here is what their conversations might contain based on the perspective of that person's gift. Which one most represents what you might have said?

1. "Here's a little gift! Now I brought your mail in, fed your dog, watered the plants, and washed your dishes." ☐
2. "I can't begin to tell you how I felt when I learned you were so sick. How do you feel now?" ☐
3. "Don't worry about a thing. I've assigned your job to four others in the office." ☐
4. "What is God trying to say to you through this illness? Is there some sin you haven't confessed?" ☐
5. "How can we use what you are learning to help others in the future?" ☐
6. "Do you have insurance to cover this kind of illness?" ☐
7. "I did some research on your illness and I believe I can explain what's happening?" ☐

Circle Your Answer Below:

Christian 1: SERVER
Christian 2: MERCY
Christian 3: ORGANIZER
Christian 4: PROPHET
Christian 5: EXHORTER
Christian 6: GIVER
Christian 7: TEACHER

WRAPPING IT UP

From today's exercises, list the answers you circled in each of the four answer keys:

1.
2.
3.
4.

Do you see a clear trend toward a single dominant gift?

Are you surprised? Explain.

Close by reading this Scripture:

Each one should use whatever gift he has received to serve others, faithfully administering God's grace in its various forms. If anyone speaks, he should do it as one speaking the very words of God. If anyone serves, he should do it with the strength God provides, so that in all things God may be praised through Jesus Christ. 1 Peter 4:10-11

Thinking about spiritual gifts, how does this Scripture change your perspective on what the Lord has given you?

Tomorrow we will spend time describing each of the spiritual gifts. If you are having trouble understanding the meaning of your gift—or if you are having a hard time narrowing it down to one—this will help you gain greater clarity. We will also look at how your gift can be used, as well as the limitations that our human nature often places upon it.

Day 5 | What Makes You Tick?

UNDERSTANDING SPIRITUAL GIFTS

God gives us spiritual gifts for a purpose. Our role is to recognize those gifts and faithfully seek ways to serve others with what He has given us. Today we are going to focus on pinpointing your dominant gift and highlight ways you can be most effective using it.

Scripture is very clear about the importance of spiritual gifts:

God gives spiritual gifts

Now about spiritual gifts, brothers, I do not want you to be ignorant.
1 Corinthians 12:1

To further your understanding, refer to Paul's writings on spiritual gifts found in Romans 12:3-8; 1 Corinthians 12:7-11; and Ephesians 4:1. Take a few minutes, review these Scriptures, and make a list of the spiritual gifts found in these three books of the New Testament:

Here is some additional insight found in these Scriptures:

All believers have at least one spiritual gift. (1 Corinthians 12:7, Ephesians 4:7)

No one has them all. (1 Corinthians 12:12, 29-30, 37)

Our areas of gifting differ. (Romans 12:3-6)

We receive our gifts according to the will of God—not our own choosing.
(1 Corinthians 12:11; Ephesians 4:7-8)

Today we are going to help you identify and confirm your dominant spiritual gift. This approach to gifting is based on our study of the Scriptures and training provided by Bill Gothard and the Institute of Basic Life Principles (IBLP).

To more fully understand the concept of a dominant spiritual gift, think back to the work you did identifying your primary personality style through the DISC profile. When the need arises, you can exhibit any of the four personality styles, but one is your strongest. One reflects your natural, factory-installed wiring. It is where you operate most comfortably and effectively. We believe the same principle applies when it comes to spiritual gifts.

According to Gothard, there are seven distinct areas of dominant spiritual gifting. They are listed in the first column of the chart below. The other two columns reflect areas of ministry where you might be called to serve and ways your gifts can be manifested and used. But, regardless of when you operate in these secondary areas of gifting, your dominant gift is still actively guiding how you interact, respond, and serve.

Classification of Spiritual Gifts

Dominant Gifts	Areas of Ministry	Ways Gifts Are Manifested
1. Prophecy	Apostles	Word of wisdom
2. Serving	Prophets	Word of knowledge
3. Teaching	Teachers	Faith
4. Exhorting	Miracles	Healing
5. Giving	Healings	Miracles
6. Organizing	Helps	Prophecy
7. Mercy	Governments	Discerning of spirits
	Tongues	Tongues

The goal today is to help you determine which of the seven dominant gifts is the one that, for you, is most important and most closely aligns with your purpose.

Looking back at the spiritual gifts inventory you completed yesterday, what area of gifting scored highest most frequently? Based on this scoring, are you able to determine your dominant spiritual gift?

Note your dominant spiritual gift here and use the side margin to jot down your thoughts about what the results might be telling you.

Extra Help:
If you're still struggling to identify your dominant spiritual gift, the charts that follow in this section may help you narrow it down. If you have already identified your dominant gift, these charts will help you understand and confirm it more fully.

Rather than using numerical rankings, we are going to have you evaluate statements based on how well they apply to you. Some of you will immediately recognize yourself, others will need to study each of the statements and pray for insight.

As with many parts of our personalities, each gift comes with positive points as well as negative potential. Once you know your dominant gift, take the time to note areas where you could run into difficulties. We encourage you to pay special attention to the section titled "Watch Out For." Awareness is the first step to being able to guard against possible weakness.

GIFTS CHARTS FOR IDENTIFYING AND CONFIRMING YOUR DOMINANT SPIRITUAL GIFT

To Identify Your Dominant Gift:
If you have not been able to clearly identify your dominant spiritual gift, highlight or put a check mark next to the statements in each of the following charts that apply to you either always or very frequently. Once this is complete, you will likely have one chart with far more marks than the others. This is a good indication that you have identified your dominant gift.

To Confirm Your Dominant Gift:
To confirm and gain deeper understanding of your dominant spiritual gift, go to the one chart for the spiritual gift you have identified as your dominant gift. Highlight or put a check mark next to the statements in that particular chart that apply to you either always or very frequently. Study this chart to learn more about yourself and how to apply your gift.

Server	
CHARACTERISTICS: • Hospitable • Alert • Available • Flexible	BLESSINGS: • Sees and meets practical needs • Frees others to achieve • Disregards weariness • Meets needs quickly • Puts "extra touches" on jobs
NEEDS & DESIRES: • Needs approval • Has difficulty saying no • Gives unrequested help • Likes short-range projects • Works beyond physical limits • Can be frustrated with time limits	WATCH OUT FOR: • Letting "things" be too important • Neglecting God-given priorities in favor of short-term issues • Resenting lack of appreciation • Impatience with other people's priorities and schedules

Prophet	
CHARACTERISTICS: • Bold • Truthful • Persuasive • Obedient	BLESSINGS: • Desires justice • Wholeheartedly involved in cause • Willing to suffer for cause • Loyal to truth versus people • Alert to dishonesty
NEEDS & DESIRES: • Needs to express himself • Makes quick impressions of people • May jump to conclusions • Reacts harshly to sinners • Feels a responsibility to correct others • Sees things in black and white rather than acknowledging shades of gray	WATCH OUT FOR: • Making decisions impetuously rather than thinking them through • Lacking tact in dealing with others • Becoming critical of both self and others for not living up to sometimes impossibly high standards

Teacher	
CHARACTERISTICS: • Self-controlled • Thorough • Dependable • Patient	BLESSINGS: • Relies on established resources • Gathers many facts • Presents truth in systematic order • Uneasy with subjective truth
NEEDS & DESIRES: • Needs to validate information • Requires thoroughness • Enjoys spending hours doing research • Checks credentials of others	WATCH OUT FOR: • Showing disrespect to people and ideas that lack credentials • Becoming proud of their knowledge • Taking teaching to extremes • Arguing over minor points • Puts mind/knowledge above the Holy Spirit

Exhorter	
CHARACTERISTICS: • Wise • Creative • Enthusiastic • Discreet • Seeks Truth	BLESSINGS: • Committed to spiritual growth • Able to see root problems • Sees necessary steps toward goal • Turns problems into benefits
NEEDS & DESIRES: • Desires to be transparent • Desires to share face to face • Overly optimistic • Likes to see facial responses • Shares private illustrations	WATCH OUT FOR: • Keeps others waiting on him • Overly proud of visible results • Treats people as projects • Gives up on uncooperative people • Starts projects prematurely • Has difficulty following through on projects

Giver	
CHARACTERISTICS: • Resourceful • Thrifty • Content • Grateful • Punctual	BLESSINGS: • Able to see resources • Invests self with gift • Exercises personal thriftiness • Hopes gift answers prayers
NEEDS & DESIRES: • Needs to give high quality • Desires to give secretly • Fears gifts may corrupt the receiver • Frugal with money for self	WATCH OUT FOR: • Hoarding resources for personal use • Using gifts to control people • Gives too sparingly to family • Gives to projects vs. people • Waiting too long to give

Organizer	
CHARACTERISTICS: • Strong • Leader • Responsible • Decisive • Loyal • Determined	BLESSINGS: • Takes initiative • Able to delegate • Able to visualize final project • Withstands reaction to tasks • Makes even complicated tasks look easy • Very alert to details
NEEDS & DESIRES: • Demands loyalty in associates • Loses interest in finished jobs • Fails to explain or praise	WATCH OUT FOR: • Views people as only resources • Delegates to avoid work • Puts projects ahead of people • Can overlook serious faults

Mercy	
CHARACTERISTICS: • Compassionate • Gentle • Attentive • Sensitive	BLESSINGS: • Sincerely loyal to friends • Empathizes with hurting people • Attracted to prophets • Deeply sensitive to loved ones
NEEDS & DESIRES: • Needs deep friendships • Desires to remove hurts • Cuts off insensitive people • Leans on emotion vs. reason	WATCH OUT FOR: • Takes up offenses, occasionally to extremes • Becomes possessive of people • Tolerates evil • Attracts people with problems • Has difficulty being decisive

If your dominant spiritual gift is still not clear, continue to ask the Lord for clarity. As He tells us in ***Matthew 7:7, "Ask, seek and knock...when you do, it will be given."*** We have found that many clients begin to see things about themselves—and their natural area of gifting—simply by being more deeply aware of the characteristics and traits outlined in these charts. Begin to pay attention to your natural preferences and tendencies and come back to these charts to see if the Lord is revealing answers in the days and weeks ahead.

A WORD OF CAUTION

Whether you are still seeking or have already confirmed your dominant spiritual gift, we want to take time now to share a thought from Pastor Bill Hybel's bestselling book *The Power of a Whisper:*

> "I caution people against running headlong into a field that is totally foreign to their "wiring patterns," their education, their expertise and their experience in life this far. It's not that God can't endorse a dramatic 180-degree turn. It's just that typically when He does so, it gets affirmed a variety of different ways."

This not only applies to your spiritual gift, but to all the work you will be doing in the **7 Steps** program. One of the beautiful parts of the process is having the opportunity to do so many different assessments in one place, over such a compressed period of time. As you proceed, it is important to remember that each piece is just one element of your mosaic. It's the collective work of art that will tell the final story—each part working in harmony with the others.

just one element of your mosaic

It does not mean that the Lord can't—or won't—do the unexpected. But if you find this happening, it is very important to walk cautiously, seek other sources of validation, and make sure you aren't jumping to conclusions or heading down the wrong path. We will talk in detail about specific methods of validation when we get to the end of the program, but for now just keep Hybel's word of caution in mind.

As Tom teaches this principle in the **7 Steps** program, he often uses himself as an example. He is a 90 percent high D with a strong spiritual gift as an Organizer. He says that if his dominant spiritual gift had somehow come out as Mercy it would've had to be a miraculous work of the Lord or a clear indication he needed to do a lot more validation!

DIVE DEEPER

If you want to learn more about spiritual gifts and the creator of the inventory you have just taken, visit the Institute of Basic Life Principles at www.iblp.org. We highly recommend their book *Understanding Spiritual Gifts*.

A more detailed spiritual gifts inventory can be done online through the same company that provides the DISC personality analysis. Both can be found in the Resources section of www.IdentityandDestiny.com.

FOCUS ON YOUR STRENGTHS AND ENJOY BEING YOU

From grade school through adulthood, we often spend a lot more time trying to correct our deficiencies than expanding upon our strengths. We want to help you change that tendency. If you are going to find, know, and live your God-given purpose, you must first discover and build on your strengths. It will help you:

- Focus on your blessings.
- Appreciate the "you" God wants you to be.
- Guard your heart and mind from envying the gifts of others.
- Allow you to put your gifts to their highest and best use.

It's not about being all things to all people—it's about being the amazing YOU God created!

WRAPPING IT UP

Let's close by remembering Bill Hybel's word of caution and taking a look at all four assessments you've completed over the past two weeks. We are going to *focus on your strengths* and tie it all together:

What are your greatest personality and behavioral strengths as identified through your DISC profile?

What are your strongest areas of resilience?

What are your top 5 core values?

What is your dominant spiritual gift and the positive character traits that come from that gift?

Are you seeing alignment? Can you find the common threads running through your answers?

What are these common threads?

What do they tell you?

Are there things you see that could be pointers to your purpose? Note them here.

Review | *What Makes You Tick?*

KEY POINTS TO REMEMBER!

- Core values are the "guardrails on the highway of life." They shape—at the deepest level—the way you respond to events in life and the choices you make. It is important to know and live by them.
- Your core values can, and should, be consciously chosen. If you choose to change them, you are then working at the level of your identity and spirituality. These are the most powerful areas for leveraging change in your life.
- The Lord gives spiritual gifts for a purpose. Your role is to recognize those gifts and faithfully seek ways to serve others with what He has given you.
- Exercising your one dominant spiritual gift allows you to experience a deep sense of personal fulfillment while achieving maximum fruitfulness and minimum weariness.
- This is a process—don't jump to conclusions too quickly. Look deeply into each piece of your mosaic as it is discovered, and remember that the real masterpiece will be revealed in step 7 when it is all pieced together.
- It is extremely important to discover and build on your strengths. It will help you focus on your blessings and be the amazing "you" God created!

be the amazing "you" God created

Your Big "Aha"
List the most dramatic and important things you discovered or learned this week.

Capture It!
Focus on thoughts, feelings, and revelations from the Lord. Go back through this week's work and capture the words, phrases, pictures, feelings, and key thoughts that have come to you and may be pointing to your purpose.

God's Word
Identify the Scripture that impacted you most deeply this week and journal your thoughts in the following format:

Write out the Scripture:

Identify its **Message** to you:

How can you **Apply** that to your life?

Write a **Prayer** back to God about this Scripture. Thank Him, ask for help, or just talk about it with Him.

Personal Notes, Thoughts, and Journaling

STEP 3 | WEEK FOUR

What's Your Passion

PASSION PURSUIT

NEEDS BENEATH THE PASSION

Day 1 | *What's Your Passion?*

PASSION: A powerful and compelling emotion or feeling—such as love or hate. A strong or extravagant fondness, enthusiasm, or desire. (www.dictionary.com)

With passion being such an intense feeling and emotion, it might seem easily identified. But in Step 3 of your journey we are going to go beyond the obvious and look for the **link between passion and purpose**. We will be helping you look below the surface and see what your passions are really telling you.

As you complete this week's "Passion Pursuit" assignment, you will be exploring your passions to find important clues to your purpose. You will be looking at:

- past events, accomplishments, and experiences
- things you want to accomplish in your life
- people who have influenced you
- wrongs you would like to make right

Unlike the other assessments you have completed thus far, you won't be scoring your Passion Pursuit at the end of each day. This questionnaire is actually going to take two days to complete. Additionally the first two days will not include the normal "Wrapping It Up" sections since each question, in and of itself, will already have you summarizing the high points of what you are learning about yourself.

As you move into the latter part of this week's work, you will not only identify your passions, but you will also discover:

- the underlying needs and desires they address
- the common threads that run through them
- the ways they point to your God-given purpose

Perhaps the best way to show you how important it is to look below the surface is to share a story:

Barry S. is a very successful businessman and leader in his church who came to Tom because he recognized that something very important was missing in his life. As they worked through the **7 Steps** program, Barry talked about his passion for flying helicopters, and said that one of his most important accomplishments was earning his pilot's license.

Delving more deeply into that experience, he discovered the real accomplishment was learning to master the technical, electrical, and physical elements necessary to fly a helicopter. He greatly enjoyed the beauty of the earth as seen through the wide lens of a helicopter windshield, but his real passion was using his God-given technical abilities to control a very sophisticated piece of equipment.

On the surface, Barry knew he had a passion for flying his helicopter, but looking more deeply, he recognized the real need behind his passion. If he had only focused on his love for flying, the insight into his purpose would have been limited to aviation. But, by identifying the need behind his passion, he opened a much larger area of exploration. He learned that his passion was not simply the art of flying—it was the mastery of difficult and highly technical challenges.

DIVE DEEPER

Many programs devoted to the search for purpose focus their efforts on the discovery of passion as the ultimate indicator of purpose. We believe passion is a vital link, but if you rely on it as your primary indicator, it can be both inadequate and sometimes even misleading. It is an important piece of your mosaic but cannot stand alone. Dive deeper by visiting www.youtube.com and searching for "Passion versus Purpose." You'll find an *Identity and Destiny* video where Tom Wolf shares some great insight into why it is so important to look beyond your passion when searching for purpose—and why it's so important to know that your passion may not be enough for success in life. Check it out.

PASSION PURSUIT QUESTIONNAIRE

Let's begin today's work with the Passion Pursuit Questionnaire, designed to help you identify the things that evoke powerful and compelling emotions or feelings of strong fondness, enthusiasm, and desire. Get ready to dig deep into your passions and see what the Lord will help you discover!

Instructions:

- The questions in this exercise are divided into two days.
- We suggest you begin by reading all 12 questions before you begin. This will give you a good overview and allow your subconscious to begin working on the questions ahead of time.
- Pray and ask the Lord for deep insight and good recall.
- Don't feel like you have to answer the questions in the exact order they are written. Use the next two days to complete the questions, beginning with those that seem easiest to answer. Come back to the others when you have had more time to think about them
- Steer clear of common experiences like weddings and births or emotional times such as sunsets or a walk in the woods. You also should avoid describing spiritual moments when you've felt very close to the Lord. Even though these are powerful experiences, we'd like for you to focus on specific times that are unique and personal to you. We want you to think deeply!

For Example:

> "In June, I was giving an acceptance speech as incoming president of our local Chamber of Commerce. I had a great feeling of confidence and anticipation in spite of the challenges we would face. I knew with certainty that all my work experience and social involvement had prepared me to lead."
>
> NOT: "I get great satisfaction when doing public speaking."

PASSION PURSUIT: Questions 1-6

1. If money and time were not obstacles, what would you do to create meaning in your life?

2. If you only had one year to live, what would you do with your time?

3. List the things you are especially good at doing.

4. As a child, what did you always want to be when you grew up?

5. When you look back at the end of your life, what will make you feel satisfied and fulfilled?

6. Describe a time when everything seemed to fall into place, obstacles were readily overcome, and you functioned at the peak of your abilities.

Day 2 | *What's Your Passion?*

PASSION PURSUIT: Questions 7-12

7. Describe specific times in the past when you felt the most positive energy and personal satisfaction.

8. If there was one "wrong" in this world that you could make "right," what would it be?

9. The Lord says our sorrow "breaks His heart." Describe a time when you felt your heart breaking over the sorrows of another.

10. Name the top three people you admire. They could be living or have passed away. What makes them so admirable to you?

11. What would you do if you knew you couldn't fail?

12. What were the three most enriching and fulfilling moments of your life?

COMMON THEMES AND THREADS

Now the fun begins!

We're going to begin by going back through your Passion Pursuit responses looking for common themes, words, and phrases. This will help you begin to peel back the layers and discover the greater needs that lie beneath your passions. Those needs and desires are important pointers to your purpose.

discover the greater needs

As you work through today's assessment, you will be looking for the themes and concepts that are important to you at a totally different level than the events and passions you've identified earlier this week.

And while you've probably spent the first two days of the week seriously considering your answers, in this section try to focus on feelings and emotions rather than rational thoughts. You don't want to "think" too hard when the goal is discovering your passion. Remember, we're looking for the underlying needs and desires that may never be identified unless you just let it flow.

We like to call passion the "light on the dashboard" of your life. The light, in and of itself, is not important. It is, however, an indicator that something important is happening—it is telling you to look under the hood. The brighter the light, the stronger the passion and the more likely there is a strong underlying need that's been identified.

For instance, many people are passionate about golf but the underlying need beyond that passion may be totally different for different people. One may thrive upon the competition and the opportunity to play a challenging game. Another may enjoy the natural beauty of a golf course and the opportunity to spend time outdoors. A third person might enjoy both of those pursuits but still discover that the most important need is the camaraderie and opportunity for fellowship with others.

The common passion is golf—the need it satisfies is quite different. Knowing your deepest needs can help you make sure that your purpose satisfies at the deepest level of your being.

LOOKING BELOW THE SURFACE

Identifying, recognizing, and addressing the needs that create your passion are strong pointers toward purpose. That is what this next exercise, called "Needs Beneath the Passion," will help you discover.

As you search for the passion and underlying need that relate to each common theme, the process of asking probing questions can really help.

For Example:

- If part of your answer to question one is "teach children to read," then ask yourself why that is important to you.
- If the answer to that question is "to make the world better for the next generation," ask why it's important again.
- If that answer is "to solve world problems one child at a time," you can begin to see the common themes of children and world betterment emerging.

Another Example:

- If part of your answer to question seven is "recognition for a job well done," then ask why that is important to you.
- If your answer is "a need for approval," then ask why that approval is important.
- It might go back to a childhood experience when you were not accepted and loved. That indicates a bedrock need—a desire for acceptance and love—that is very different from your original response.

NEEDS BENEATH THE PASSION

Instructions:
As you work through this assessment, focus on common themes and concepts. Look for words, patterns, and places where you can see the interrelationship between the questions and your responses.

- Go back through all your answers in the Passion Pursuit questionnaire and highlight or underline the common themes that can be found. List them in column one on the next page.
- For each theme, identify the passion it evokes and list it in column two.
- For each theme and related passion, list the underlying need in column three.

1. Common Themes	2. Passion	3. Underlying Needs
Time with family and friends	Showing love for those I care about	A desire for deep connection

MORE THAN PASSION

This latest exercise goes through what is sometimes called a "reverse process" of discovery. It would be very difficult to start by asking you to define your deepest needs. But hopefully coming at it from a different direction has helped you see them more clearly. First, you had to identify the common themes and then the resulting passions they evoked. Most importantly, you had to look beyond the passion to find the underlying need.

This process is designed to help you uncover things about yourself that may not be readily seen or known. It's all there in your subconscious—it may just take a little work to find it.

What has this exercise helped you discover that you found most surprising?

Were you able to identify passions that were actually indicators for bigger, and possibly far more important, needs?

Do you see how your needs may be pointing toward your purpose? Explain.

DIVE DEEPER

Again we have arrived at one of those places where experience shows that having a trained coach can help optimize your experience. We encourage you to visit the Resources area of www.IdentityandDestiny.com and learn more about the coaches who have completed our certified training programs and the "laser coaching" sessions we've created to target specific concerns without requiring a long-term commitment. Custom-designed services provide the help, support, and encouragement you need. All inquiries are strictly confidential. (Coaches are available by telephone or Skype so geographic location is not an issue.)

PLEASE NOTE: If you would like information on becoming an *Identity and Destiny* Certified Program Leader, please contact us at www.IdentityandDestiny.com.

WRAPPING IT UP

While the emotions are still running strong, spend another 10 minutes reviewing your answers in today's "Needs Beneath the Passion" exercise. Look for words and themes that really resonate—sometimes even causing a physical reaction. Make note of them below. Words that cause the strongest reaction are important pointers to your true purpose and can be essential tools when you begin creating and verifying your purpose statements.

Day 4 | *What's Your Passion?*

ONE MORE LOOK AT PASSION

Today we want you to take a final look back and review your answers in the two exercises you completed this week: "Passion Pursuit" and "Needs Beneath the Passion." But this time, we'll make the focus of your review the things that have given you the greatest joy, satisfaction, passion, and fulfillment!

Based on this review and everything you have learned this week, create a list of seven statements that finish the sentence:

I feel excited and passionate when I am... ______________________.

Begin each statement with an action word, such as "having," "enjoying," "working," "spending time," etc.

Some examples:

...having the chance to learn and use new knowledge

... being part of a committed and focused team

...helping others mature spiritually

...spending true quality time with my family

...sharing intimate and meaningful conversation with someone I care about

...inspiring others to reach for something greater in life

I feel excited and passionate when I am...

1.

2.

3.

4.

5.

6.

7.

BRINGING IT ALL TOGETHER

You've spent the last three weeks completing what is probably the most intense and in-depth examination of your personality you will ever take.

You've looked at your:

- Primary Personality Style
- Resilience Quotient
- Top 5 Core Values
- Dominant Spiritual Gift
- Passion Pursuit and Needs Beneath the Passion

Each instrument and assessment you've competed is individually informative but together they paint a picture that none of them alone can present.

If you've sincerely worked these first three steps, you're sure to have begun learning a lot about yourself and your God-given character, gifts, and passions. As management guru Peter Drucker said:

> "Success in the knowledge economy comes to those who know themselves, their strengths, their values, and how they best perform."

Take a moment here to write down the five most important things you've discovered—the hidden strengths, character traits, and blessings you hadn't recognized or fully acknowledged before you started **7 Steps to Purpose:**

PHASE 1 COMES TO AN END

Interestingly enough, our research shows that most purpose programs would now be ready to wrap things up. They would have you writing your purpose statement based on what we consider the first phase of the process!

Programs such as these are based strictly on an intellectual search for purpose. They rely on the philosophy of a "self-created" purpose, and the idea that meaning in life can be found through self-analysis. They say, "All you have to do is look inside yourself to find your destiny."

God

is the

creator

We have a different philosophy!

We clearly value intellectual analysis and put great emphasis in Phase 1 on knowing how you are created and wired. But we are now ready to go beyond self-analysis. You will soon begin the process of going to God—your Creator—to get His revelations about the plans and purpose He has for your life.

I know the plans I have for you, declares the Lord. Jeremiah 29:11

For God's gifts and his call are irrevocable. Romans 11:29

We believe God is the Creator and ultimate source of wisdom regarding your purpose. He's had it planned from the very beginning:

All the days ordained for me were written in your book before one of them came to be. Psalm 139:16

The word of the Lord came to me saying, Before I formed you in the womb I knew you. Before you were born I set you apart. Jeremiah 1:4-5

REMEMBER OUR ANALOGY

With the **7 Steps to Purpose**, you are still in the early stages of collecting the beautiful pieces of your purpose mosaic. It is far too early to start jumping to conclusions about your purpose. There is still more work to be completed as we help you reach out to the Lord for His wisdom, guidance, and revelation about your identity, destiny, and assignment.

WRAPPING IT UP

Have you ever spent time asking the Lord to reveal the plans He has for your life?

Why or why not?

If yes, how did you go about doing that? What was the result?

If yes or no, what brought you to the point of wanting to do it now?

Whatever brought you to this point, we believe there is no more important work you could be doing than this!

Psychological studies show that unless we make a conscious decision to do otherwise most of us tend to follow the path of least resistance, a path that leads to a life that simply seems to happen. So, if you want to find your God-given purpose, it's going to take intentional effort and focus. It's going to require being "purposeful" about finding your purpose. And:

- The Lord will honor your effort. There is no doubt He has something special planned and He wants you to discover it.
- You will enter the will of God and experience supernatural peace, energy, and joy.
- You will be doing what the Lord would most like to see you do. What could be more pleasing to the Lord than that?

So we make it our goal to please Him…For we must all appear before the judgment seat of Christ, that each one may receive what is due him for the things done…whether good or bad. 2 Corinthians 5:9-10

Day 5 | What's Your Passion?

WHAT'S NEXT???

Before we continue collecting the pieces of your mosaic, we are going to spend time in the coming week getting rid of a few things you won't need to carry with you anymore. In Step 4, we will help you work through any fears, blocks, or limiting beliefs that may stand in your way. We will also help you cross over "the bridge" from the analytical to the emotional, intuitive, and spiritual parts of your discovery process.

This step is where the "pedal meets the metal." This is where you will be going beyond conscious analysis to your spirit—your very heart and soul—to discover who you are and why the Lord put you here.

the Lord uses everything

For some, this soul-searching will be very challenging because we will ask you to look into the past and events that you might rather forget. We will also ask you to shut down the judgmental, critical, and skeptical parts of your psyche, and this too can be difficult as you shift gears and begin working at the level of emotion rather than intellect.

But, do not fear. Don't put on the brakes and stop now. We will be with you every step of the way. We'll make sure you are able to safely navigate this phase of the journey. We will help you see why this is such a critically important and beneficial part of the **7 Steps to Purpose**.

Do not let your hearts be troubled. Trust in God, and trust also in me. John 14:1

THERE'S PURPOSE IN THE PAIN

One of the basic underlying assumptions of the **7 Steps to Purpose** is that the Lord uses everything that happens in our lives: the good, the bad, the uplifting, and even the ugly. They're all part of building the attitudes, character, skills, and abilities that you need to execute His purpose for your life.

For those of you who've had very tragic or difficult things happen in your life, this may be hard to comprehend or accept. But, please, take a moment to think about this from the Lord's perspective:

God promises that He will comfort you when you mourn, and provide for you when you grieve. He will bestow on you a crown of beauty instead of ashes. He will take the parts of your life that lie in a heap of rubble and transform them into something beautiful. He will help you rebuild the ancient ruins of your life and restore the places long devastated. He will give you the power to renew that which has been ruined and devastated for generations. (Paraphrased from Isaiah 61:3-4)

Only a loving, caring, all-powerful God can do that!

As you grapple with the idea that the Lord can (or would even want to) make anything good out of your rubble and ashes, keep in mind that God is not the one that caused the bad things to happen.

beauty out of ashes

The truth is this: We live in a broken and sinful world where truly tragic and indescribable things happen. But, in spite of the things that have happened to you—or you may have caused by your own mistakes and sin—the Lord is there to bring you through it! He is ready and able to help you find ways to bring glory out of your tragedy.

If you put your eyes on the Lord and trust Him—regardless of your circumstances—He can bring beauty out of ashes and is...***able to do immeasurably more than all we ask or imagine...to him be the glory...forever and ever! Amen. Ephesians 3:20-21***

Now, if you will allow yourself to internalize and believe this truth, you will be able to apply a whole new perspective to the negative experiences of your life. Is that easy? No! But when you do, your life will take on new meaning.

Take the time to read Isaiah 61 in its entirety. Think about what God is saying to you in this Scripture and complete these sentences.

God is...

God will...

I need God to...

God is your comforter, provider, rebuilder, and restorer. He is your salvation and righteousness. He is your sovereign Lord.

Will you allow this truth to change your heart and your perspective? Will you allow the Lord to give you a new attitude of faith and confidence? Note your thoughts:

see and trust the providential hand of God

Remember: Every circumstance, event, person, and encounter in your life has the potential for good when placed in the all-powerful hands of the Lord. What may have been meant for harm, God can use for good. God can use it all!

The life of Joseph, as chronicled in the latter chapters of Genesis, shows this truth as well as anywhere in Scripture. In **Genesis 50:20**, Joseph says to his brothers who had tried to kill him: ***"You intended to harm me, but God intended it for good to accomplish what is now being done, the saving of many lives."***

Once you embrace this kind of attitude, we hope you can begin to see the trials of life as a way of gaining the strength, wisdom, empathy, and usefulness that might not be achieved any other way. If you hadn't gone through those experiences, you might never be equipped to execute on your purpose in the way that you are now prepared. So, as we've said before: Whatever you do, don't waste your pain!

If you are going to find, know, and live your purpose, you will need to learn to see and trust the invisible, yet providential hand of God in every part of your life.

THERE'S ONLY ONE YOU!

There is one more assumption we want to share with you as you move into the next phase of the **7 Steps to Purpose.** We want you to recognize that the purpose the Lord has for you belongs to you and you alone. God created you as a unique individual to fulfill a unique purpose and nobody else can accomplish what He has planned for you to do!

This is not to say that the sovereign will of God for all mankind will be thwarted if you don't do your part. On the contrary, the Lord tells us clearly:

That which I have planned, I will do! Isaiah 46:10

But He does have plans that YOU are perfectly created to fulfill. If, in the power of your own free will, you choose to ignore them, then that's your choice. God will accomplish all that He has planned. But know this: the Lord eagerly and passionately waits for you to accept His invitation to play your part!

That's why the **7 Steps to Purpose** are so very important! If you never bothered to seek the Lord and learn your purpose, you would miss not only the extraordinary blessings He has planned for you in this life, but the eternal rewards waiting in the next.

The man who plants and the man who waters have one purpose, and each will be rewarded according to his own labor. 1 Corinthians 3:8

Behold, I am coming soon! My reward is with me, and I will give to everyone according to what he has done. Revelation 22:12

A DIFFERENT WAY OF LOOKING AT THINGS

As we come to the close of this week's work, let us challenge your thinking one last time.

Many Christians have been taught that "God is God and you are not." We are taught from an early age that life should not be self-centered and "all about me." But when it comes to purpose, let us suggest that perhaps there is a time when it is all about YOU!

This change in our thinking became particularly clear as we were studying the story of Jesus and Peter in Chapter 21 of the book of John. If you aren't familiar with this passage of Scripture, or haven't read it in a while, we suggest you read John 21:15-23.

In this awesome demonstration of love, Jesus is taking Peter through a process of forgiveness and reconciliation for the three times Peter had denied knowing Him on the eve of Jesus' death. Throughout their conversation, Peter is expressing his love and devotion, while Jesus is giving Peter specific directives regarding the purpose He has for his life: "Feed my lambs, take care of my sheep, and follow me!"

Amazingly, in the very next verse following this intimate exchange, Peter looks over and asks Jesus: "What about John? What do you have planned for him?"

Now, we know this line of questioning did not take Jesus by surprise but His response shows that this was a real "teaching moment" between Peter and the Lord. Jesus answers by asking: "What is it to you, Peter?"

In other words, Jesus said, I have just given you the purpose I planned for your life. Now, get on with it and don't worry about John or anyone else. It is not about them, it's about you. Focus on what I've asked you to do and don't worry about the purpose I have for others!

Wow!!!

How often do you worry more about what the Lord has for someone else?

How often do you want what the Lord has given someone else?

How often has the Lord given you instruction and you have chosen to look the other way?

Could this possibly be the case with your purpose in life, just as it was for Peter?

Can you imagine how Peter must have felt when he had denied Christ three times, yet Jesus still chose him to be instrumental in spreading the gospel and building His church? What would have happened if Peter had denied the purpose Jesus planned for him? What if Peter had minimized the potential for greatness that Jesus saw in him? What could that mean in the context of your life and your purpose?

WRAPPING IT UP

Another week is complete. Great job!!!

Savor what you have learned and remember:

You are one-of-a-kind, uniquely designed, and created by God. He has something very special planned for you!

Regardless of what you have done—or what has happened in your life—the Lord can weave redemption out of your mess and glory out of your tragedies. Everything that has happened in your life can be used as a valuable part of your purpose.

glory out of tragedies

God created you perfectly for the purpose He has planned. It's your job to recognize that immutable fact, face any obstacles that stand in the way, and diligently work to discover your purpose.

Let's carry on, shall we?

Review | *What's Your Passion?*

KEY POINTS TO REMEMBER!

- Steps 1 to 3 have been like a "CAT scan" of how you are wired, looking at your strengths, skills, values, gifts, needs, and passions to provide valuable insights and important pieces of your purpose mosaic.
- Passion is a vital link to purpose but if you rely on it exclusively it can be inadequate and perhaps even misleading.
- The needs that lie beneath your passion are strong pointers toward purpose. It is important to identify and understand those needs.
- God is the Creator and ultimate source of wisdom regarding your purpose.
- Finding your God-given purpose takes intentional effort and focus. It requires being "purposeful" about finding your purpose.
- What may have been meant to harm you, the Lord can use for good.
- Whatever you do, don't waste your pain!

Your Big "Aha"
List the most dramatic and important things you discovered or learned this week?

Capture It!
Focus on thoughts, feelings, and revelations from God. Go back through this week's work and capture the words, phrases, pictures, feelings, and key thoughts that have come to you that may be pointing to your purpose.

God's Word
Identify the Scripture that impacted you most deeply this week and journal your thoughts in the following format:

Write out the Scripture:

Identify its **Message** to you?

How can you **Apply** it to your life?

Write a **Prayer** back to God about this Scripture. Thank Him, ask for help, or just talk about it with Him.

Personal Notes, Thoughts, and Journaling

STEP 4 | WEEK FIVE

What's Stopping You?

ROADBLOCKS TO PURPOSE

FEARS, BLOCKS AND LIMITING BELIEFS

SMOOTHING A PATH TO PURPOSE

Day 1 | What's Stopping You?

Congratulations! You've completed Phase 1 of your journey. This week you will move through Step 4 and finish Phase 2 in its entirety. We often refer to this step as "the bridge" of the **7 Steps to Purpose**. It's only one step, but it is critically important. It is where you will transition from the intellectual and analytical parts of the program to exercises that will be done on a deeper, more emotional, intuitive, and spiritual level.

You are now embarking upon what we believe is the most important part of finding your purpose—going directly to your Creator to ask for it. After all, how can you know what you were created to do without going to the one who drew the blueprint?

For you created my inmost being; You knit me together in my mother's womb. I praise you because I am fearfully and wonderfully made; Your works are wonderful, I know that full well. Psalm 139:13-14

But before we get too far ahead of ourselves, we need to spend some time getting rid of the fears, blocks, and limiting beliefs that might hinder your progress. We also want to help you be fully prepared to hear God's voice when He speaks. This week, we are going to look at issues that, if left unaddressed, could prevent you from finding your purpose and becoming the person the Lord intends you to be.

SEVEN ROADBLOCKS TO PURPOSE

If only the path to purpose were clear, direct, and obvious. But, unfortunately, that's seldom the case. Most often, what we see is a road filled with bumps and turns, questions and doubts.

Over the years as we've worked with clients to help them find their purpose, we have come to expect roadblocks on the path to purpose. Take a careful look at these seven major roadblocks and identify which issues are most likely to cause you to stumble.

ROADBLOCKS TO PURPOSE

Instructions:
Read through this list, then rank the following seven roadblocks in order of their importance. Use a scale of one through seven with seven being the least of your concerns and one being your greatest obstacle.

_____ **Satisfaction:** Life is pretty good the way it is, I'm not sure I'm willing to rock the boat.

_____ **Complacency:** It's just not worth it to carve out the time to reprioritize my life. I'm not sure I'm willing to make the effort to find and live my purpose.

_____ **Unbelief:** I'm not sure God really has a plan for my life. I'm not certain there is anything special enough about me that the Lord would want to use me.

_____ **Fear:** I'm afraid of what my purpose is going to require of me. I'm not sure I'm ready or willing to face the questions and choices I might have to make.

_____ **Procrastination:** I just can't take on another project right now, maybe later when the other things that are demanding attention in my life are more under control.

_____ **Unwillingness:** I would rather not know. If God gives me my purpose, then I'll be responsible for acting on it. I'm not sure I want to disrupt my life with all that.

_____ **Unworthiness:** I can't believe that the Lord could use someone like me. My past has surely doomed my future. There is no way I can be of any use to God.

What was your biggest obstacle and why is that roadblock your greatest concern?

HERE'S WHAT WE HAVE FOUND:

Based on our work with hundreds of clients over the past five years, FEAR is the biggie! If fear was not the top issue for you, it's likely to be near the top of your list. Nearly everyone who has completed the **7 Steps to Purpose** has had to face some type of fear as a roadblock. When it comes to finding your God-given purpose, fear raises its ugly head in so many different ways:

WHAT IF...

- I don't like my purpose?
- I have to make big changes?
- The risk or the cost is too high?
- It's not important enough?
- I'm not up to my purpose?
- I have to give up something that's important to me?
- I am wrong about my purpose?
- I can't find my purpose?
- I'm rejected or ridiculed?
- I fail?
- I'm not qualified enough?

Do any of these fears ring true for you? Highlight the fears you think are most likely to become problems.

We will be taking a deeper look at fears in the week ahead. The important thing now is your willingness to name your fears.

More About What We Have Found in Working With Clients:
Another major roadblock is unworthiness. So many people are secretly living with such deep shame, guilt, regret, and sadness that it blocks them from any sense that their lives could be of value, especially in the eyes of God.

May we get personal for a moment?

Is there any part of you that wonders if God could possibly want to use you—given your choices, mistakes, and things that have happened in the past?

Stop and think about that for a few minutes and then consider what God has to say. All you need to do is take a look at the numerous examples in the Bible to see how the Lord has often used the most unlikely, the most ordinary, and the most sinful people to do extraordinary things for Him. Let's start by looking at some of these people, including several who Jesus chose to be His closest disciples.

We talked about Peter in the last section. He was a simple fisherman with an impetuous nature who often found himself in trouble with the Lord. Then there was Matthew, a tax collector. He was considered among the worst of sinners and was hated by all but those in the government who profited from his work. Even Paul, who wrote 13 epistles, confessed to having "violently persecuted" Christians before his conversion on the road to Damascus.

TREASURE IN YOUR PAST

Author and Bible teacher Beth Moore says in her destiny-filled study of Esther:

> "There is treasure in your past that God wants to put square in the middle of your destiny. And contrary to what you might think or feel, God has chosen you for a specific purpose—not in spite of your history, but because of it!"

treasure in your past

Pastor Chris Hodges at Church of the Highlands in Birmingham, Alabama recently shared this quote from the movie *Seabiscuit*:

> "God never throws a life away because it is a little banged up!"

WRAPPING IT UP

Now take a few moments and think about how our biblical examples and these two quotes might apply in your life. Answer the questions below and see what the Lord can show you about how He might want to use things that you would rather hide or forget.

Can you think of failures, disappointments, or struggles in your past that God has used or could use in a positive way? Describe.

How might those things point toward your purpose?

What's your greatest fear about finding your purpose? Why? (Remember: just naming it is your first step in overcoming it.)

Do you see ways your past failures or disappointments could be preparing you to help other people—particularly those you might not otherwise relate to?

Day 2 | What's Stopping You?

BATTLE FOR THE SOUL

As we prepare to move forward with this week's work on fears, blocks, and limiting beliefs, we're going to take a little side trip on our journey.

WARNING: FOREWARNED IS FOREARMED!

Today's detour is all about readiness. We want you consciously aware and prepared for the kind of things you are likely to confront in the days and weeks ahead.

something wonderful in store

As you move into the spiritual parts of discovery and begin to ask the Lord to reveal your purpose, there will be things in addition to your fears, blocks, and limiting beliefs, that get in the way. They can be far more subtle but equally important.

You are likely to find life's little problems becoming more difficult and consuming. You may find yourself plagued with busyness and having far less time for your **7 Steps** homework. You may even find yourself feeling like there are forces that really don't want you to discover your purpose, forces that don't want you to begin living the life God has planned for you. Be aware. There is an unseen spiritual world that has power. It is no match for the power of the Lord, but it can give you a tough time.

Finally, be strong in the Lord and in his mighty power. Put on the full armor of God so that you can take your stand against the devil's schemes. Our struggle is not against flesh and blood, but against the rulers, against the authorities, against the powers of this dark world and against the spiritual forces of evil in the heavenly realms. Ephesians 6:10-12

You are also likely to see your basic human nature starting to get in the way. Since we are all creatures of habit, you may find yourself wanting to maintain the status quo. You may begin to resist the idea of leaving your old familiar comfort zones. As you seek the Lord for your purpose, you might begin to say, "Wait a minute, what kind of change is this going to involve?" You may begin to feel reluctant to explore what lies ahead.

Here's the plan:

- Know interference will come.
- Pray! Ask the Lord for wisdom, protection, and strength.
- Be prepared. You may just have to muscle your way through these obstacles and keep putting one foot in front of the other.
- Trust God! Know He has something wonderful in store.

- Be ready to replace reticence with anticipation.
- Replace concerns with the expectation that God has places of promise, victory, and purpose waiting.
- Your job: Stay the course and finish strong!

Remember what we've been telling you from the beginning:

You do the steps—God does the rest.

Stay steady, work through the issues, and place your faith in the Lord and His Word:

So, do not fear, for I am with you, do not be dismayed, for I am your God. I will strengthen you and help you; I will uphold you with my righteous right hand. Isaiah 41:10

A DIFFERENT KIND OF BATTLE

Now, let's take a look at what's going on when we talk about interference. It's really about the battle that Scripture says is going on inside each of us—it is the battle for your SOUL.

Unlike epic tales of medieval battles and knights wielding swords, this is not a war that is won or lost at any particular moment in time. It is an ongoing battle with two fierce opponents: your BODY and your SPIRIT. They continue their battle day in and day out. In practical, everyday terms, it can be seen in struggles as difficult and complicated as truly forgiving someone who has wronged you or as simple as choosing not to share a juicy piece of gossip with your best friend over a cup of coffee.

Take a look at the diagram on the next page for a visual explanation of what we are talking about.

As you look at this diagram, remember that the Lord tells us that we are made in His image (Genesis 1:26). And, just as God is triune (three parts), so are we. God is Father, Son, and Holy Spirit. We are body, soul, and spirit.

For God, there is no conflict in the triune nature of who He is. But for us, the story is quite different. In Genesis Chapter 1, God gives the details of original sin and the fallen nature of man that resulted from that sin. Since that time, the battle for man's soul has been raging.

For the sinful nature desires what is contrary to the Spirit, and the Spirit what is contrary to the sinful nature. They are in conflict with each other, so that you do not do what you want. Galatians 5:17

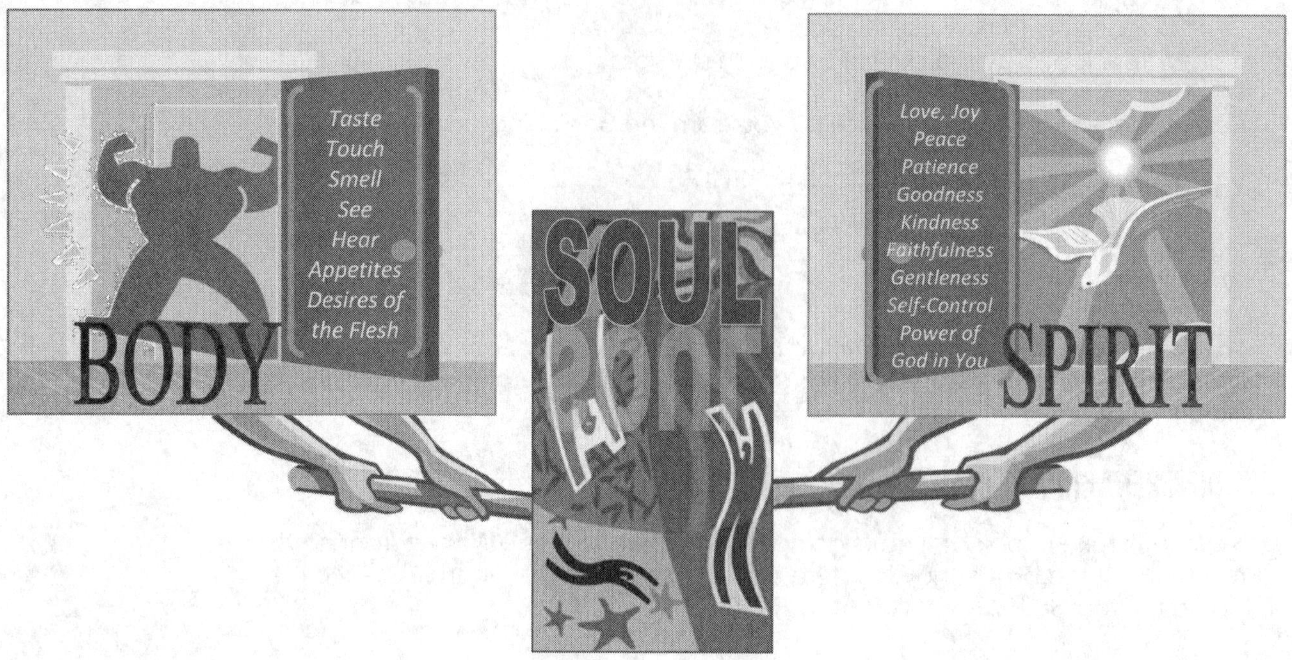

THE SOUL IS YOUR MIND, WILL AND EMOTIONS - IT IS THE BATTLE GROUND!

Both the Body and Spirit strive to be in command of your soul. You have the power to choose which door to open to fulfill your desires. When one door is closed, the other opens as a floodgate. To which side will you submit your soul in this tug-of-war, the body or the spirit?

Galatians 5:16-17 – So I say, live by the Spirit, and you will not gratify the desires of the sinful nature. For the sinful nature desires what is contrary to the Spirit, and the Spirit what is contrary to the sinful nature. They are in conflict with each other, so that you do not do what you want.

NOTE: What moves the Soul out of peace? Fear!

I John 4:18 – There is no fear in love. But perfect love drives out fear, because fear has to do with punishment. The one who fears is not made perfect in love.

Hebrews 2:14-15 – Since the children have flesh and blood, he too shared in their humanity so that by his death he might destroy him who holds the power of death – that is, the devil – and free those who all their lives were held in slavery by their fear of death.

NOTE: Death can be physical, identity, financial, emotional etc.

THE THREE PARTS OF MAN

- **The Body**: the sinful servant of your fallen human nature that possesses all of mankind's carnal cravings, lusts, wants, and desires. Also called the flesh or sinful nature.
- **The Soul:** your mind, will, and emotions. This is the battleground! This is where you have choices. You can choose the power and ways of the spirit or acquiesce to the desires of the body.
- **The Spirit:** the innermost, immortal part of your being. Every person—believer or non-believer—is made up of body, soul, and spirit. And Scripture tells us that when you become a reborn believer, God's Holy Spirit actually comes to dwell in your spirit. God can then manifest His nature through you, giving you the "fruit of the spirit" that produces love, joy, peace, patience, kindness, goodness, faithfulness, gentleness, and self-control in your life. (See Galatians 5:22.)

YOUR BATTLE PLAN

As you reflect on these three parts of man and the battle for your soul, think of it as a heads-up for what lies ahead. As we move into work that is done spiritually rather than analytically, we will be asking you to surrender to the power of the Holy Spirit.

The most common area of conflict is between your intellect or mind and your desire to surrender to the Spirit. Your intellect will say things such as, "this makes no sense," or "I want to be in charge," and "you can't really hear the voice of the Lord."

All the while, your desire to surrender will be saying, "seek the Lord," and "yield to the power of the Spirit," or "relax, trust, and listen for the Lord."

Have you begun to feel any kind of interference? Explain.

Internal conflict is normal. When you begin to ask your intellect to take a back seat to your spirit, resistance will come. But don't be fearful. We just want you to be forewarned and prepared. Awareness is the first step. Spiritual preparation is step two. We recommend putting on the armor of God as described in Ephesians 6:10-18.

Take a moment now to look up this scripture, read it, and make a few notes below on the proactive things you can do to win this battle. It is all about the Lord's power, but it is interesting to note the one offensive weapon that God shows us in this Scripture is the sword, which is His Word. There is power in the Word of God to defend yourself and win this battle.

YOUR CHOICE

If at any point in this process, you become fearful, uncertain, or skeptical, then your soul will begin to feel the repercussions. You might find yourself wondering why you ever started looking for purpose. You may doubt the entire process. Questions like "Am I going to have to give up my comfortable lifestyle or my own agenda?" are likely to pop up in your mind, perhaps even to the point of dominating your thinking. You may even be looking to the Lord saying, "Whoa! This isn't what I bargained for. This is not what I had in mind!"

This also is normal. That's why Step 4 is so important!

If those kinds of thoughts are allowed to grow, you will feel increasingly uneasy and out of balance. And when your soul lacks peace, your very nature will suggest you do nearly anything to get it back into balance! The question is, how will you choose to do that?

Your body will say: "Eat this for comfort, drink that to medicate, buy something you know you can't afford. Quit this process NOW and go back to 'normal' etc."

the victory

is yours

But, if you are prepared and willing to persevere, your spirit in concert with the Holy Spirit will say: "Be wise and seek the Lord to find the kind of peace that lasts. Find the purpose the Lord has for you and live the abundant life that the Lord has in store."

Why spend money on what is not bread, and your labor on what does not satisfy? Listen, listen to me, and eat what is good and your soul will delight in the richest of fare. Isaiah 55:2

The battle is certain, but with the Lord's help, the choice—and thereby the victory—is yours. Body versus spirit: to which opponent will you relinquish the battle ground of your soul?

With your help I can advance against a troop; with my God I can scale a wall. As for God, his way is perfect; the word of the LORD is flawless. He is a shield for all who take refuge in him. For who is God besides the LORD? And who is the Rock except our God? Psalm 18:29-31

WRAPPING IT UP

Take a few moments and reflect on the battle we've described today.

Are you experiencing or can you remember experiencing this kind of struggle? Write about it here.

How can you use what you've learned today to win this battle? How can you respond to the power of the spirit rather than the desires of the body?

Are you ready and willing to surrender to the power of the Spirit as you go forward discovering your God-given purpose? YES ____ NO ____

If your answer is NO, please commit to praying that the Lord will change your heart as we continue to work in this area of yielding to the power of the Spirit. Take time now and pray for the willingness to truly surrender.

Day 3 | What's Stopping You?

FEARS AND CONCERNS

Over the next three days, we are going to do some very important work as we gaze directly into the face of your fears, blocks, and limiting beliefs. But there's good news: we're not going to leave you alone to face down those foes. We are going to help you smooth a pathway through them as we show you how to neutralize their power and impact.

According to *Webster's Dictionary*, fear is: "A painful emotion or passion excited by an expectation of evil or the apprehension of impending danger. It is an uneasiness of mind, focused upon the thought of future evil likely to befall us."

Another definition is: **F**alse **E**vidence **A**ppearing **R**eal

No wonder we don't like fear! And it's no surprise that it can be so debilitating!

But take the time now to study these definitions. Can you see that fear is defined more by emotions, thoughts, and a state of mind than real danger?

We are not here to question the legitimacy of your fears or belittle your concerns. Our goal is to help you identify and think clearly about them. We want to help you be able to move beyond them and live without that burden.

DO NOT FEAR

As you work through this section, remember what Franklin Delano Roosevelt said as he was inaugurated during the worst economic depression the world has ever seen: "The only thing we need to fear is fear itself."

Fears are natural. They are part of the human condition. But we can become enslaved to them, accommodating a comfort zone that keeps us from achieving our full potential. As you embark upon what will probably be the most challenging part of the **7 Steps to Purpose**, remember three things:

1. You cannot move beyond your fears, blocks, and limiting beliefs until you change the way you think about them.
2. You cannot change your way of thinking without new information.
3. Your source of new information must be one you consider valid.

We suggest that you turn to the Lord and His truth as given in the Bible as your valid source. In the next few days we will be showing you specific ways to do that.

POWER OVER FEAR

We have the privilege of worshiping at one of the fastest-growing churches in the state of Florida under the direction of senior pastor Matthew Hartsfield. He often reminds us: "The phrase 'do not fear' appears at least 365 times in Scripture—that's once for every day of the year."

God obviously knows this is an area of weakness and wants us to turn to Him rather than allowing fear to stop us in our tracks.

face your fears

There is one passage in Deuteronomy that has often helped us do exactly that:

The Lord himself will go before you and will be with you. He will never leave you, nor forsake you. Do not be afraid; do not be discouraged. Deuteronomy 31:8

Wow! Picture that: The Lord going ahead of you, making a clear path, and promising to be with you every step of the way.

We can't tell you how many times we have prayed that Scripture as we've faced a frightening situation. By putting our minds on the Lord's promises rather than our circumstances, a God-given sense of peace, calm, and assurance has overtaken our hearts and minds just when we've needed it most. The Lord also promises:

Do not be anxious about anything, but in everything, by prayer and petition, with thanksgiving, present your requests to the Lord. And the peace of God, which passes all understanding, will guard your hearts and your minds in Christ Jesus. Philippians 4:6-7

We invite you to memorize these verses and use them both as spiritual weapons and a source of comfort and reassurance. You will be amazed by their power.

FACING YOUR BIGGEST FEARS

Today's exercise will help you identify fears that may stand in the way of finding, knowing, and living your God-given purpose. You must face your fears if you are going to overcome them.

Once they're in writing, then we can address them one by one, acknowledge them, and seek the Lord's wisdom to help you neutralize your emotions and gain clear, rational thinking. This is all part of keeping the desires of your body and flesh from sabotaging the process. It will allow you to win the battle for your soul, safely move beyond your fears, and find the purpose the Lord has for your life.

But before we begin, we want you to take time to reflect on your goal and the benefits to be gained as you move forward in your process of purpose discovery.

Looking deep into your heart and soul, why do you want to know your God-given purpose?

What positive changes are you hoping this will make in your life?

With these benefits in mind, let's get to work removing anything that might get in the way of being able to discover your God-given purpose!

IDENTIFYING YOUR FEARS

Instructions:
Pray and ask the Lord to help you list ALL the fears, reservations, and concerns you have about finding and living your God-given purpose. Be bold and honest with your list and know that we all experience fears and concerns. The important thing is how you choose to think and react to them.

Go back to the list of fears you worked on in Day 1 of this week and review it carefully. Be sure to list whatever comes to mind, big or small. Don't consider anything insignificant.

Start your list below, but know it is unlikely that you will complete it in one attempt. You will want to add to your list in the days ahead. Jot things down as they come to mind.

My List of Fears:

With your fears identified, we are now going to begin addressing them. Start by remembering our definition of fear:

False **E**vidence **A**ppearing **R**eal

This next process is designed to help you see your fears rationally and realistically. It will allow you to put them into perspective and prevent your fears or concerns from becoming an emotional stop sign on your path to purpose.
We'll use a process called Future Pacing that takes your fears to their wildest extreme. This will help you see that most of what you fear will never actually happen. It will also help you establish limits or boundaries that can provide the protection you need to keep moving forward.

Most importantly, it will allow you to face your fears and wrestle with the truth that the Lord is faithful. If the "worst thing" did ever happen, what we all need to know and remember is God loves us, He will take care of us and He is sovereign.

We like to call fear a "caution sign" on the highway of life. When you see those alongside the road, remember they're warnings and not stop signs. The fear you feel may indicate an area of your life where you should slow down and pay attention to potential danger, but you don't have to come to a screeching halt.

Fear can cause you to be so cautious and careful that you protect yourself right out of your destiny. As you work through this exercise, remember the goal is to turn false evidence into a more realistic view of things. Now, let's remove this roadblock called fear.

SMOOTHING A PATH THROUGH FEAR

Instructions:
Use a separate piece of paper to record your answer to the following questions for each of the fears you choose to work through.

1. Review your list of fears and select the one that seems to hold the most power and emotion. Remember, these are fears related to finding your purpose, not day-to-day fears like insects or airplanes.

2. Future Pace this fear by asking yourself: What is the worst that could happen if that occurred? Write down the answers.

3. Continue to go deeper into your fear by repeating the second question several times. Note your thoughts and feelings.

4. Knowing this, ask yourself: Am I willing to look past this fear and go forward with the Lord's plan for my life?

   If the answer is "yes," then you have—perhaps for the first time—looked at this fear honestly and rationally. You have been able to look beyond your emotions and false assumptions, and you have smoothed a path through your fear.

If the answer is "no," ask yourself the following questions:
(a) What is the probability of this fear causing my worst-case result?
(b) What are the real ramifications of this happening?
(c) Is it realistic to put my life's purpose on hold based on this fear?

setting boundaries

Based on these answers, can you now say "yes"?

If not, think about this:
(a) You have the gift of free will—you have a choice.
(b) You can put boundaries on how far you are willing to go.
(c) You can put limits on the changes you are willing to make—and the things you will or won't do.

5. Make a note of any limits or boundaries that would be required for you to comfortably move forward with the plans the Lord has for your life.

6. Repeat this exercise with all the major fears on your list. You can also continue to use this same process if old fears you've dealt with reappear. (Note: Usually your list of fears can be grouped into less than three major categories—you may express them in many ways but they generally fall into just a few broad groups.)

Whether it is setting boundaries or taking a realistic look at your fears that allows you to move forward, that is what we are working to help you achieve. It's about smoothing a path through fear and being able to confidently move forward in finding your God-given purpose.

A THOUGHT ABOUT BOUNDARIES

Caution: Don't get too hung up on this idea of setting boundaries with God. God is sovereign, in control, and has a specific plan for your life. And guess what? If you have fears, He already knows about them and wants you to bring them to Him. He wants your honesty. He understands your needs. He knows what you can handle and what you can't.

If you need to set a limit on how far you will go so you can safely move forward in this process, then we have no doubt that He will meet you right where you are. Then, over time, if the Lord wants you to move beyond a boundary that's been set, we believe He will prepare you and help you peacefully make that change.

May the God of peace...equip you with everything good for doing his will, and may he work in us what is pleasing to him, through Jesus Christ. Hebrews 13:20-21

And with many of us, the Lord's process of "equipping" and preparation takes time. Your job now is to be honest with yourself, lay your limits before the Lord, and be willing to do what you can. God will do what you cannot.

It's funny how this one basic truth keeps showing up—but here it is again:

You do the steps—God does the rest!

WRAPPING IT UP

Well done!

Has today's exercise helped you identify your greatest fears? Are you surprised by any of them? Note your thoughts.

Are you gaining confidence that you can overcome your fears—put them into perspective—and move forward into the purpose-filled future the Lord has planned for you? Explain.

Remember: This technique of Future Pacing fears is a tool that can be used whenever you find yourself up against a roadblock that's stopping your forward progress in life.

Day 4 | What's Stopping You?

BLOCKS THAT HINDER

Hopefully you are beginning to make real progress when it comes to smoothing a path through your fears. If you are still struggling, please continue to work with yesterday's tools and trust that the process can, and does, work. It may just take a little more time and effort.

Today we're going even deeper as we look at your blocks. And although this may be tough to hear, if you are not in right relationship with your Creator, you are likely to be blocked (in part or in whole) from hearing His voice.

Surely the arm of the LORD is not too short to save, nor his ear too dull to hear. But your iniquities have separated you from your God; your sins have hidden His face from you, so that he will not hear. Isaiah 59:1-2

Thankfully, our God is long-suffering and slow to anger. He is anxious for you to seek Him and surrender the things that are holding you back. We call these "blocks." They will stifle what the Lord wants to do in and through your life if you leave them unaddressed.

Today's exercise has two parts: First, we will help you identify your blocks. Secondly, we will show you how to remove them.

IDENTIFYING YOUR BLOCKS: PART 1

To find your blocks, take a moment and ask yourself the following list of questions. But, before starting, you might want to think about the reality that our blocks are in place because we often cannot see the truth. Ask the Lord to help reveal the truth as you think about your answers:

What is the one thing in the world that I just can't seem to give up?

What is a higher priority in my life than it should be?

What am I striving for that seems to be consuming me?

What am I holding on to so tightly that it is creating stress and problems?

What am I overly anxious, frightened, or worried about?

What am I consumed by? (i.e., job, image, ambition, or finances)

What fills me with the need to control other people and circumstances?

God is faithful

What am I hanging on to that is hurting me and others? (anger, unforgiveness, lust, addictions)

REMOVING YOUR BLOCKS: PART 2

Our experience has shown that you must be willing to do the work necessary to get into right relationship with the Lord before He will speak clearly about your identity, destiny, and assignment. It doesn't mean that you need to conquer every block completely; it just means you need to show the Lord you are ready to begin taking the steps. The ultimate removal may take time, but what we have seen is this: God knows your heart and He will honor your willingness to surrender your blocks and be obedient to what you know is right. The key word is willingness!

Looking back to Part 1, some of you may have been able to quickly identify your blocks. They are clear and present every day—you just haven't gotten around to removing them. Others of you may not be sure if you have blocks or how to identify them.

As we start this process, we need to tell you that it's not complicated but it can be difficult—especially if you're not ready to yield your will to the Lord. Sometimes the hardest part is letting go. We'll provide more resources later if you still need help, but let's start now with prayer.

Step 1: Awareness: Let's begin by praying the following psalm. Ask the Lord to make you aware of anything that is blocking your relationship with Him.

Search me, O God, and know my heart; test me and know my anxious thoughts. See if there is any offensive way in me, and lead me in the way everlasting. Psalm 139:23

Step 2: Confess to God: Your next step also is clearly laid out in Scripture:

If you confess your sins, God is faithful and just and will forgive your sins and purify you from all unrighteousness. 1 John 1:9

Confession literally means "to speak sameness" or to "agree with God." It is more than saying you are sorry. It means being honest, and then getting right with the Lord by agreeing with Him about the nature of your sin and the need to remove any blocks He reveals.

Won't you pray and ask the Lord to help you do that right now?

Step 3: Confess to Others You might also need to consider the steps that the Lord lays out in the book of James:

Therefore, confess your sins to each other and pray for each other so that you may be healed. James 5:16

God is the only one who can forgive sin, but the healing we need may only come when we confess and pray with one another.

If you are finding this difficult to understand or put into practice, let us share some further insight regarding this Scripture from the study notes in the *Life Application Study Bible (NIV)*:

> "Christ has made it possible for us to go directly to God for forgiveness. But confessing our sins to each other still has an important place in the life of the Church. If we have sinned against an individual, we must ask him or her to forgive us... If we need loving support as we struggle with a sin, we should confess that to those who are able to provide that support... If, after confessing a private sin to God, we still don't feel His forgiveness we may wish to confess that sin to a fellow believer and hear him or her assure us of God's pardon."

Take time now for some deep introspection about what you need in these areas of forgiveness and healing. Go to the Lord in prayer and ask Him what you need to do. If it would help to journal or make a few notes on what needs to be done, do that in the side margin as a way to hold yourself accountable.

Finally, always seek godly counsel from your pastor or other mature Christians if you have any doubt about how you should proceed. And keep in mind the caution that is part of the AA Twelve Steps:

> Step 9: "Make direct amends to such people whenever possible, except when to do so would injure them or others."

ONLY GOD

Sometimes the work you need to do can only be done by the Lord. Perhaps the reason your blocks are still in the way is because you have tried to deal with them on your own. Maybe you are not letting the Lord do what only He can do. Or, you simply aren't genuinely ready to "let go and let God."

Here is a thought to consider from *Experiencing God Day by Day,* by Henry Blackaby:

> "Satan will try to convince you that obedience carries much too high a price. But he will never tell you the cost of not obeying God."

everything

that hinders

THE CHOICE IS YOURS!

We don't know your blocks—but we suspect that you do. And, if you don't, the Lord will reveal them if you continue to ask.

The most important question is this: Do you really want to do something extraordinary for the Lord with your life?

If you are like the vast majority of people, the answer is a resounding YES!

If so, the next question is this: Will you remove the blocks that hinder you?

Let us throw off everything that hinders and the sin that so easily entangles, and let us run with perseverance the race marked out before us. Hebrews12:1

What hangs in the balance could be the "kingdom-size" purpose the Lord has planned for your life. You don't want to miss out on that, do you? Begin removing your blocks and getting into right relationship with the Lord so you can clearly hear His voice and live the purpose He has planned.

DIVE DEEPER

We often recommend Beth Moore's series entitled *Praying God's Word: Breaking Free From Spiritual Strongholds,* available as a book and audio CD as well as a daily devotional. She addresses 14 major strongholds including bitterness, anger, and unforgiveness, showing readers how to replace them with the mind of Christ and fervent daily prayer. We welcome you to visit the Resources area at www.IdentityandDestiny.com to order your copy.

WRAPPING IT UP

Take a few moments to reflect on what today's work has revealed. Along with the work you have committed to doing in the areas of forgiveness and healing, journal your thoughts and begin to talk with God about all that He wants to uproot and remove from your life.

Day 5 | *What's Stopping You?*

FEAR'S FIRST COUSIN—LIMITING BELIEFS

As we worked on fear, you learned the definition:

"**F**alse **E**vidence **A**ppearing **R**eal."

When that kind of false evidence turns into false beliefs about your abilities and self-worth, it will, in one way or another, keep you from achieving your dreams. False beliefs place serious and unnecessary limits on what you believe about your potential and what you can accomplish. Fear is no longer just fear—it has transformed into what we call "limiting beliefs."

you are good enough

Limiting beliefs are usually deep-seated in your subconscious. They are so subtly tucked into the way you see yourself that you don't realize the impact they are having on your life. Most people don't recognize these self-imposed limits. They are unaware of how these negative beliefs influence the way they make decisions and see their possibilities.

Although limiting beliefs may manifest themselves in many different ways, they almost always fall into two broad categories:

1. What if I'm not good enough?
2. What if there is no one to take care of, or care about, me?

Scripture is very clear in answering both of these two questions:

First, the Lord created you perfectly. He did so with a specific purpose in mind and then gave you the talents and skills needed to fulfill that purpose.

If God loves you that much, do you really need to worry if parents, bosses, friends, or siblings think you're "good enough"?

In fact, you need go no further in the Bible than the first chapter of Genesis to see what God has to say about the "crown jewel" of His creation: ***Let us create man in our own image, in our own likeness. Genesis 1:26***

And, when God saw what He had made, He said: ***It was very good. Genesis 1:31***

Without a doubt, you are good enough! In fact, you are made in the very image of God Himself.

Secondly, if your concern is who will take care of you, the Lord has already addressed that too. Jesus promises that God knows when even a sparrow falls and has counted the hairs on your head (Matthew 10:29-30). He knows exactly what you need when you need it—and will provide it! In the Psalms, God spells it out quite clearly:

The Lord will keep you from all harm—He will watch over your life; The Lord will watch over your coming and going both now and forevermore. Psalm 121:7-8

You can trust that the Lord cares about you and will take care of you. He is the one you can depend on—now and forevermore!

LIMITING BELIEFS BY ANOTHER NAME

Limiting beliefs are deep-seated, subconscious, and based on false evidence and assumptions. What's another name for that? We would call it a lie. Today, we'll work together to help you replace your limiting beliefs, or lies, with the truth, God's truth as found in Scripture.

IDENTIFY THE LIES AND THE CAUSE

Instructions:
Begin by finding a quiet place to do this exercise, get comfortable, then go through the following list of lies and limiting beliefs. Read them out loud and highlight the statements that resonate with you—the ones that give you a strong emotional or physiological reaction when you read them. (Don't worry about completing the cause right now, we'll come back to it in a minute.)

Limiting Beliefs or Lies	The Cause
I'm not smart enough.	
I'm not good enough.	
I can't handle failure.	
I don't know how to deal with my mistakes.	
I'll never get what I want.	
I'm worthless.	
I'm selfish.	
I'm a fake...a pretender.	
I'll never be able to change.	
I can't handle success.	
My past has doomed my future.	
I'm not worthy.	
I'm not capable.	
I'm a failure.	
I'm ______________	

Fill in the blank, and prayerfully add any other limiting beliefs to this list—whatever comes to mind.

Now that you have identified your limiting beliefs, we want you to begin looking at them with the mind-set that they are indeed lies that need to be replaced.

Replacing your lies with truth is a two-step process presented in the form of a two-part equation. Before you start, let us show you the equation and give you an example:

Equation Part 1: The Lie

______________________________	=	______________________________
(1) My Reality or the Cause		(2) My Limiting Belief That Resulted

Equation Part 2: The Truth

______________________________	=	______________________________
(3) God's Truth on This Matter		(4) My New Empowering Belief

An example of the two-part equation:

Equation Part 1: The Lie

(1) I came from a divorced family =
(2) I am an outcast and will never be valued

Equation Part 2: The Truth

(3) I am adopted into God's family, chosen, and cherished (Eph. 1:4-6) =
(4) I am a child of God and have great value

Now, before we work on the equations, go back to your list of limiting beliefs and try to identify the cause for each belief you listed. Write it in the column titled "Cause" next to the applicable limiting belief.

As you begin to identify the events, circumstances, or experiences that caused your limiting beliefs, you will need to think back over your life. This may not be easy, but it is a very important part of the process. Identifying the cause and then being able to look at it objectively is a big part of going from an old subconscious, emotional reaction to a new conscious, truth-filled belief.

As you search for the cause, look at your life in total, the past and the present. Experience shows that many of our strongest limiting beliefs come from some sort of childhood wounding. It could be as simple as a harsh word or single act of unkindness or it could be something much more serious.

The goal here is not to point fingers or cast blame, just to look for causes and try to understand their impact. Only then can you begin eliminating the power they have over your life. You can look to God for His healing power and truth that will allow you to have a choice about what you believe. When you believe the Lord's truth about the matter, you can gain the strength and freedom needed to leave the lies behind.

Are you ready to replace your lies with truth? Are you ready to be empowered by the truth—and free to be all the Lord has planned? The next exercise is designed to do just that.

you have
a choice

REPLACING YOUR LIES WITH TRUTH

Instructions:

1. For Equation 1: From the list you created earlier today, start with the limiting belief that seems to be your strongest. Enter that in blank (2) of the equation: My Limiting Belief That Resulted.
2. For Equation 1: Next, fill in blank (1) with the cause from your list.
3. For Equation 2: Then you will fill in blank (3) with God's truth. The source is Scripture. Start with the concordance in the back of your Bible. Look for words that relate to the specific areas where you need help. Using a concordance is a great way to look for Scripture that's applicable to your particular situation. Another good resource is www.biblegateway.com. In the back of this workbook, we have also provided a list of all the Scripture referenced in this book. Many people find applicable Scripture for this exercise there.
4. For Equation 2: Finally, you will fill in blank (4) with the belief that, based on the Scripture in blank (3), you now know God wants you to have. The path to freedom is based on replacing your lie with God's truth and these new empowering beliefs. You will then have a new way of looking at reality—a reality as seen through the eyes of God.
5. Repeat this exercise for each of the beliefs that are limiting you from finding and living the abundant, free, and powerful life God has planned for you!

Equation Part 1: The Lie

______________________________ = ______________________________
(1) My Reality or the Cause (2) My Limiting Belief That Resulted

Equation Part 2: The Truth

______________________________ = ______________________________
(3) God's Truth on This Matter (4) My New Empowering Belief

Equation Part 1: The Lie

____________________ = ____________________
(1) My Reality or the Cause (2) My Limiting Belief That Resulted

Equation Part 2: The Truth

____________________ = ____________________
(3) God's Truth on This Matter (4) My New Empowering Belief

Equation Part 1: The Lie

____________________ = ____________________
(1) My Reality or the Cause (2) My Limiting Belief That Resulted

Equation Part 2: The Truth

____________________ = ____________________
(3) God's Truth on This Matter (4) My New Empowering Belief

truth
will set
you free

Equation Part 1: The Lie

____________________ = ____________________
(1) My Reality or the Cause (2) My Limiting Belief That Resulted

Equation Part 2: The Truth

____________________ = ____________________
(3) God's Truth on This Matter (4) My New Empowering Belief

Congratulations! You have done some deep—and perhaps difficult—work today. Your courage and tenacity will be rewarded. Truth is the only sure path to freedom.

Then you will know the truth, and the truth will set you free. John 8:32

WRAPPING IT UP

How to Make Change That Lasts
As part of completing your equations, you were asked to identify Scripture that can help you change your beliefs. If you want to make change that will last, you will need to refer to those verses regularly and allow God's truth to sink deep into your heart and soul (mind, will, and emotions).

Be transformed by the renewing of your mind. Romans 12:2

Write your Scriptures out and either memorize them or keep them on index cards that are easily and quickly accessible. Read them as many times each day as you can. This will retrain your mind and give you the weapons you need to genuinely conquer your limiting beliefs! Remember God's Word is your sword. Come out swinging whenever you see your limiting beliefs creeping back in and taking control.

Safely Over the Bridge!
This has been an intense week. Thanks for hanging in there and crossing the bridge over what may have felt like some pretty treacherous waters. Let's go now and find a place of peace and rest with the Lord as we close in prayer:

> **Dear Father in Heaven,**
>
> **Thank you for being with me this week. Thank you for Your presence and Your protection. Thank you for all You are doing in my life through this program. Thank You for bringing me here and helping me remove my fears, blocks, and limiting beliefs. Please, Lord, remove my lies and replace them with Your truth. I trust that You can and will accomplish this in me.**
>
> **Amen.**

The Lord is near to all who call on him, to all who call on him in truth. Psalm145:18

DIVING DEEPER

Step 4 is a place where a **trained coach** may be able to help optimize your experience. If you feel "stuck in place," we encourage you to visit the Resources area of www.IdentityandDestiny.com and learn more about "laser coaching" sessions that target specific concerns without requiring a long-term commitment. (Coaches are available by telephone or Skype so geographic location is not an issue.)

If you need some extra help, we suggest that you consider **one-on-one counseling**, a recovery program like Celebrate Recovery, or a deliverance ministry. We've included a list of national resources on our website at www.IdentityandDestiny.com, and we also encourage you to meet with your pastor to discuss your concerns and get referrals to organizations closer to home as you take the necessary steps to work through any deep psychological issues or wounds that go beyond the scope of this program.

Review | What's Stopping You?

KEY POINTS TO REMEMBER!

Fears, blocks, and limiting beliefs have the power to stop you in your tracks. Here's how to eliminate them:

- Identify and expose them.
- Bring them into the light of day and consciously address them.
- Go to God and His Word for the truth.
- Replace the lie with truth. (Memorize it, keep it on an index card, and say it out loud over and over until you own it.)
- Get started on the path to freedom.

Our goal has been to help you realize—at both a conscious and subconscious level—that your fears and limiting beliefs are almost always far less frightening than they first appear. We want to help you put your fears and roadblocks in proper perspective as you face them head-on.

Peace I leave with you; my peace I give you. I do not give to you as the world gives. Do not let your hearts be troubled and do not be afraid. John 14:27

I can do everything through Christ who gives me strength. Philippians 4:13

Your Big "Aha"
List the most dramatic and important things you discovered or learned this week.

Capture It!
Focus on thoughts, feelings, and revelations from the Lord. Go back through this week's work and capture the words, phrases, pictures, feelings, and key thoughts that have come to you that may be pointing to your purpose.

God's Word
Identify the Scripture that impacted you most deeply this week and journal your thoughts in the following format:

Write out the Scripture:

Identify its **Message** to you.

How can you **Apply** this to your life?

Write a **Prayer** back to God about this Scripture. Thank Him, ask for help, or just talk about it with Him.

Personal Notes, Thoughts, and Journaling

STEP 5 | WEEK SIX

Can You Hear God Speaking?

PRAYER OF COMMITMENT

DREAMS

PURPOSEFUL PRAYER

MEDITATION

Day 1 | Can You Hear God Speaking?

YOUR MOST IMPORTANT ACTION STEP

Even after finishing all the exercises in Step 4, you may feel like you still have some work to do to successfully replace your old beliefs with new ones. Don't be concerned—this is often the case.

As you think about making these changes, you might want to keep this quote from author and preacher Joyce Meyer in mind: "An empty space is the devil's playground."

If you remove the lie, you must keep replacing it with the truth of God's Word. Keep reading, repeating, and internalizing the Scripture you identified in Step 4. The process of renewing your mind takes time. Persist with your efforts and trust the Lord to make the necessary changes. God clearly wants you guided by His truth. There is no doubt He will help you make it happen.

You do the steps—God does the rest!

For now, before you move on to the final phase of *Identity and Destiny,* we want to give you one more tool to help you move beyond any barriers that remain. We want to start Step 5 with the most important action step of all: your personal Prayer of Commitment.

In all likelihood, you are doing this program because you have a deep desire to know your life's purpose and do what the Lord has planned. You genuinely want to make a difference and leave a legacy that counts. But to do that, you must first make sure the path is clear and your heart is ready.

That is why we ask you to be thoughtful, yet fearless, when it comes to the prayer we are going to lay out for you today. Our years of experience have clearly shown that it is those who make a conscious choice to seek the Lord with all their hearts, minds, and souls who get the deepest and most enduring breakthroughs.

Until you are willing to surrender and submit your will to the Lord, your efforts will be half-measure and produce far less than possible. If you truly want to connect with your Creator and know your purpose, you must choose to "let go and let God."

So, let's get started, shall we?

Please read and study the following prayer as you prepare your heart and mind for genuine surrender:

Dear Lord:

I come to You praising and thanking You as my Creator. You are mighty, powerful, holy, and sovereign.

I humbly seek You, asking forgiveness for any unrepented sin in my life and for Your revelation of the sins I do not recognize or acknowledge. Cleanse me, oh Lord, and guide me in Your righteousness.

Today, Lord, I offer myself to You.

I pray that You will reveal my purpose; that You will guide, direct, and use me according to the identity, destiny, and assignments You have for my life.

Whenever and wherever You see my stubborn self-will interfering with Your plans, I ask that You free me from that bondage.

Take away any obstacles that will keep me from the purpose You have for my life.

I pray that living my life according to Your purpose will produce the results you desire and bear witness to Your power, love, and glory.

Having given much thought to this prayer, I am ready. Help me finally abandon myself to You.

May I do Your will always.

Amen.

(Inspired by Step 3 from AA's Big Book)

FULL CONSIDERATION

As you consider this prayer, you might want to think about the following quote from Celebrate Recovery's founder, John Baker:

> "We need to change our definition of willpower—will power is (or should be) the willingness to accept God's power. This happens when we see that there is no room for God if we are full of ourselves."

Will you let go and accept God's power? Will you trust the Lord? Will you commit to seek and follow God's will?

When you are ready, when you agree that the words of this prayer reflect the desire of your heart, please go to the Lord and let Him know you are willing to change your definition of willpower, abandon "self-will," and go forward in His.

Are you ready to pray this prayer of commitment? If so, please do that now.

A MEMORIAL OF REMEMBERANCE

Just as when the Lord had the Israelites place stones as a memorial when they finally crossed the Jordan River into the Promised Land, we ask that you sign and date the space below as a reminder and memorial of this important moment between you and the Lord when you prayed your personal Prayer of Commitment.

These stones are to be a memorial to the people of Israel forever. Joshua 4:7

Name_________________________________ Date ________________

NOW, WE CAN GET STARTED!

Beginning today, your journey of discovery is going to take you to a whole new level of depth and intimacy with the Lord. Put on your seat belt and get ready for the culmination of all you've done to this point.

a whole new level of depth

In the final three weeks of **7 Steps to Purpose**, you will learn to use five highly effective spiritual disciplines and seek the Lord directly regarding your purpose. As you turn to the Lord and ask "Who am I?" and "Why am I here?" you will learn to listen, recognize, and know His voice.

The secret to hearing God's voice? Well, it's not really a secret at all. It is simply your willingness to draw near to Him and sincerely seek what He has to say.

Come near to God and he will come near to you. James 4:8

Hopefully, the process of drawing near and seeking the Lord has already begun. You already may have asked Him to help in the discovery process as you've worked through the intellectual assessments of Steps 1 through 3. And in Step 4, you undoubtedly were turning to the Lord as you searched for truth in His Word and worked through your fears, blocks, and limiting beliefs.

But now, let's go even deeper.

Perhaps you are already accustomed to the kind of intimacy that allows you to clearly hear the Lord speak. But, statistics tell us that most of you are not. In fact, many participants get to this point and find themselves wondering, "Is it really possible to hear God speak?"

And, if He does, they say, "How do I know it's Him? How do I know I'm not just making this up or imagining things?"

First, you must know, there is no magic formula. And, although there are a rare few people who have actually heard the audible voice of the Lord, we have not. But that doesn't mean He hasn't spoken. It does not mean we haven't heard His voice. We have!

there is no magic formula

When the Lord is speaking, it is most often through the guidance and direction of the Holy Spirit. He uses a feeling, an impression, a thought, or a single word that seems to flash into your mind and just won't go away. Some Christians call it "prompting." It is not likely to be a booming voice or a full paragraph of complete sentences that fully address the issue. But it is likely to produce a clear sense of "knowing" that this is coming from the Lord. It is something you can learn to recognize, pay attention to, and ultimately, look forward to enjoying.

But when he, the Spirit of truth, comes, He will guide you into all truth. He will not speak on his own; He will speak only what he hears, and He will tell you what is yet to come. John 16:13

Rest assured, God speaks and you can learn to hear His voice!

BUT...FIRST THINGS FIRST

Hearing God's voice is almost always contingent upon the depth of your relationship with Him. As you think about learning to hear God's voice, consider the close relationship between a sheep and his shepherd.

He calls His own sheep by name and leads them out...and His sheep follow him because they know His voice. John 10:3-4

There are many places in Scripture where the Lord refers to Himself as the shepherd and us as His sheep. How comforting to have our Lord tell us so clearly that when we know our shepherd, we will also know His voice.

To have that kind of closeness, you must first invest time and energy into the relationship. Think about your closest friend, someone you love to spend time with. You have intimacy and trust that's grown out of time spent together. You've made a concerted effort to know and care for one another. You feel safe sharing not just your doubts and fears but your hopes and dreams, the deepest desires of your heart.

Your relationship with God is no different!

Remember:

- If you do not spend time with the Lord, if you do not invest in the relationship, there can be no real intimacy.
- Without real intimacy, there is little assurance that you will hear His voice.

- It won't be that's He's not speaking but because you're not slowing down long enough to listen.
- You must slow down and stop allowing the cares of this world and your daily priorities to crowd Him out of your life.

HEARING GOD'S VOICE: READY, WILLING, AND SURE

In *The Power of a Whisper*, Bill Hybel writes:

> "Hearing from God is not like receiving a text message or reading an email....Even though God's whispers are rarely tangible, there are concrete steps we can take to help discern if we are hearing from God, or hearing from the bad sushi we ate the night before."

Combining our personal experience with the teachings of Bill Hybels, Joyce Meyer, Craig Hill, and Henry Blackaby, we offer the following three steps to help you discern the voice of the Lord. The 14 points contained in these steps will help make sure you don't confuse what you are hearing with "bad sushi" or anything other than a genuine prompting from the Lord:

(I) PREPARATION: Am I ready?

(II) LISTENING: Am I willing?

(III) CONFIRMATION: Am I sure?

I. PREPARATION: Am I ready?

- Are you spending time with the Lord? Are you carving out time on a daily basis to pray and read the Bible? What are you doing to really get to know God and learn who He is? It is only through regular time with the Lord that you will get to know, trust, and love Him. It is only then that the lines of communication can really be open.
- Is your heart and mind ready?

  Do not conform any longer to the pattern of this world, but be transformed by the renewing of your mind. Then you will be able to test and approve what God's will is—His good, pleasing and perfect will. Romans 12:2

  If you want to hear the Lord's voice and know His will for your life, you must spend time in the Word, allowing it to transform your mind and prepare your heart for obedience.

- Have you decided ahead of time that you will obey? Henry Blackaby says: "If you settle ahead of time that you will obey whatever God says, you will be ready to hear His voice." God knows your heart, and if you do not intend to do what He asks, He may very well remain silent.

Proper preparation requires that you and the Lord settle this matter of obedience first. Scripture shows us over and over again that blessings almost always follow obedience.

- Can you keep your mind, will, and emotions from getting in the way? There are three interferences we want to caution you about. We call them the "three amigos." They are the critical, skeptical, and judgmental parts of your psyche. They love to get in the middle of this process and override your heart and spirit. Just as we said in Step 4, be aware of this potential interference and consciously move it to the side while you work this process. Critical evaluation has its place. But as you are striving for spiritual discernment, it is better not to allow this kind of filtering. It can block your ability to hear the unexpected ways that the Lord may choose to speak.

the floodgates opened

The Crystal Box
Let us tell you about one of our first Identity and Destiny clients. She was a very intelligent, successful, driven woman, a high "D" on the DISC, and a classic Action Hero! With her logical, take-charge personality, she was quick to allow the "three amigos" to rule the process. Over and over again, she would say she was not hearing from the Lord, and if she did hear anything, she would not allow herself to believe it was really Him.

After several sessions of trying to help this Action Hero deal with her interference, we finally found something that worked. On a table in Pam's office was a crystal box half-filled with seashells. Tom said, "Take that box, hold it in your lap, and have a little conversation with your judgmental, critical, and skeptical parts. Tell them you appreciate how they look out for you, but right now they need to take a little break. Tell them to get in the box and close the lid…tightly! Assure them they can come out when you are done, but for now, they need to simply allow you to let things flow. If they sneak out, put them back in the box and carry on."

Our Action Hero began using a box of her own and found that she was able to relax just long enough for the spiritual disciplines to begin to produce real results. Once she got a taste of what it was like to hear God's voice, it was almost as if the floodgates were finally opened. In the weeks that followed, the Lord gave her powerful insight into her identity and destiny—and one very specific assignment—all of which have changed her life dramatically for the better!

If you can get a visual on this and consciously decide that you will not allow your freedom to be hampered, you will be amazed by the effectiveness of this technique. If you have any hope of allowing your heart and spirit to get into the driver's seat as we move forward, you will have to intentionally turn off your critical, skeptical, and judgmental parts of your mind.

II. LISTENING: Am I Willing?

- Are you approaching God ready to listen rather than talk? Our prayers can often be one-way monologues, with the Lord barely getting a word in edgewise. Being quiet may seem difficult at first, but once you learn to stop and just wait for God to speak, you will be amazed at what can happen.
- Have you asked God to help you with any unbelief? Are you having a hard time really believing that the Lord can, and will, really speak to you? If so, take a few moments and think about the father who asked Jesus to heal his son in Mark 8:23 when he said, "I believe; now help me with my unbelief!" This kind of faith is not something you can obtain on your own—it is a gift from the Lord. Spend time in prayer asking Him to give you the gift of faith, help with your unbelief, and allow you to proceed with the rightful expectation that you will hear His voice.
- Are you ready to seek the Lord and then seek Him some more? Your diligence is a must. According to Hebrews 11:6, there are two very important requirements in this process of seeking the Lord. First, "you must believe that God exists" and you must believe that He "rewards those who earnestly seek Him." It is a journey. It takes time and effort. Believe, seek, and listen—God will speak.
- Are you able to listen with your heart and spirit? Learn to quiet yourself and truly listen. Find a quiet place in nature or a spot in your home where you can close out distractions. Wherever it is, use it consistently for your daily time with the Lord. Be creative in finding your special place. Early morning before anyone else wakes up gives you more options than later in the day. Over time, it will become precious to both you and the Lord if you make a habit of meeting with Him there. For you to have any chance of really listening deeply, you must find a way to stop the noise and get away. In this crazy-busy world, it is a welcome thought to do as it says in the Psalms:

God's Word is your litmus test

Be still and know that I am God. Psalms 46:10

Once you begin hearing the Lord's voice, there is one more very important step in the process. You must confirm what you are hearing.

III. CONFIRMATION: Am I Sure?

- Have you confirmed it with the Word? You must always check what you are hearing against the truth of Scripture. You must ask yourself if there is anything about what you are hearing that is not in alignment with what the Lord says in the Bible. God will never tell you to do anything that is in contradiction to His holy character or His Word. This is the single most important element of confirmation—it is your litmus test for validation.
- Have you considered your circumstances? Another way that the Lord confirms His promptings is our circumstances. Is the Lord lining things up in a way that your circumstances verify or reinforce what you are

hearing? You can call it coincidence or you can believe that is God simply choosing to remain anonymous. It may seem like the Lord is staying hidden, but He will often give you important confirmation of what He is saying through your circumstances.

- Have you sought the counsel of others? We all have blind spots and fall in to the trap of hearing what we want to hear. That is why it is very important to go to others who are wise and mature in their faith. Ask for their objective wisdom, guidance, and insight regarding what you are hearing. This is a wise and valuable part of your validation and confirmation process.
- Have you asked God directly? Take whatever you are hearing and go back to the Lord in prayer. Ask him to confirm what you think He is saying. Ask Him for His ESV: Elaboration, Specification, and Validation. We will be teaching you more about this in Step 7 when you create and validate your purpose statements. But for now, these three words are good to use when asking the Lord for His direct confirmation of what you are hearing.
- Have you considered your "wiring"? How does what you are hearing line up with what you have learned about yourself in Steps 1 through 3? Does it use anything you uncovered in Step 4? If so, this can be strong, positive confirmation. It does not mean that the Lord won't call you to something that does not fit your wiring, but if He does, you need to affirm it in lots of different ways. We believe God wired you the way He did for a reason. He allowed the events of your life for a purpose. In almost every case, He expects to put them to good use.
- Have you asked these final questions? Is what you are hearing wise according to the Lord's standards? Are you being impetuous or taking matters into your hands? Are you following your own desires rather than waiting on clear guidance from the Lord? To be sure of your answers, Lysa TerKeurst, author of *What Happens When Women Say Yes to God,* says ask yourself: "Would what I'm hearing please God?" She says asking this one final question helps remove your resistance to doing what you're told or doing something you might regret. TerKeurst says: "Always seek to err on the side of pleasing God!"

err on
the side of
pleasing
God

WRAPPING IT UP

I. PREPARATION

What is the most important step you need to take as you prepare to hear God's voice?

What is your action plan for making this happen?

II. LISTENING

What do you need to do to improve your ability to listen to the Lord?

How do you plan to make that happen?

III: CONFIRMATION

Finally, what will you do to confirm what the Lord is saying to you?

What can you put in place to have your confirmation process ready when you need it?

And as you prepare to hear the Lord speak, remember this acronym: **A–S–K**

Ask and it will be given, **Seek** and you will find, **Knock** and the door will be opened. Matthew 7:7

Day 2 | Can You Hear God Speaking?

PURPOSEFUL PRAYER

meet face-to-face with God

As we mentioned yesterday, you will be working with five different spiritual disciplines over the next two weeks. We'll start with three this week—purposeful prayer, meditation, and dreams—and then incorporate the other two in Step 6.

While we will introduce one new discipline each day, we want you to consider this a cumulative process. We ask that for the duration of the program you continue to work all the disciplines you've been taught. Taken together, they give you five unique ways to ask your Creator about your purpose. Each discipline offers a different method of reaching out to the Lord and asking for His clear direction.

We hope that you will spend at least an hour every day asking God to speak to you through these disciplines. We hope you will make this a priority and spend the time necessary to maximize the value of your time with the Lord. For most people, that's significantly more time than usual, particularly since the focus will be on "what God wants to say to you" versus the more typical "what you need from God."

CARVING OUT THE TIME

If you haven't gotten in the habit of getting up early to spend time with the Lord, know that it's going to be more important than ever going forward. Think about it this way: What if someone were to call and tell you they could get a 60-minute appointment for you to meet—face to face—with the God of the universe? This time would be exclusively yours and you could talk with Him about absolutely anything. What would you say? What would you do?

Well, you already have that opportunity and you don't even need an appointment! Please don't take this privilege for granted.

If you're already in the habit of spending time with the Lord and have a routine that you follow each day, we suggest that you replace it for the next few weeks with the disciplines we will be assigning. If you have time for both that's great, but most people find that replacing their current study or devotion time is necessary to focus on the work we will be asking you to do.

And while combining all these disciplines may sound like a lot of work, this week's three disciplines really fit together quite nicely. Purposeful prayer can be part of your quiet time, Meditation can be very effectively practiced as you walk, run, or bike outdoors. As for dreams, you get to do that one while you sleep.

SPIRITUAL DISCIPLINE 1: PURPOSEFUL PRAYER

Instructions:

1. Pick a time when you are not rushed or stressed. Find a quiet place where you will not be disturbed to create a peaceful atmosphere.

2. Have a pen or recording device so you can capture the Lord's message.

3. Get into a suitable posture for prayer.

4. After a few deep breaths, and having arrived with your mind and heart in a respectful state, begin to ask questions.

5. Open by asking: "Lord, may I speak with you today?"

6. Ask about your Identity: "Lord, what is my identity?" Wait and listen. If you get a thought, ask clarifying questions.

7. Ask about your destiny: "Lord, what is my destiny?" Wait and listen. If you get a thought, ask clarifying questions.

8. Ask about your assignment: "Lord, do you have an assignment for me?" If you get a thought, ask clarifying questions.

9. Record any words, phrases, feelings, thoughts, ideas, or pictures you receive in the space provided.

10. Close with a prayer of thanks regardless of whether or not you received anything.

11. Try to stay away from the tendency to judge, edit, modify, paraphrase, etc. Just record what you receive as you receive it. (Space for your notes is provided in the "Wrapping It Up" section at the end of each day.)

FOR FUTURE REFERENCE: You will be prompted in the days ahead to continue using this discipline. There will be many opportunities to seek the Lord for answers through purposeful prayer. We recommend that you tab this page of instructions with a sticky note or bookmark so it is easy to come back and review.

Now, take time to seek God in purposeful prayer as outlined above and record your findings in the "Wrapping It Up" section at the end of today's work.

THE PURPOSE OF PRAYER

Before we press on, let us ask, "How did the first day of purposeful prayer go for you?"

If you didn't seem to get much of anything, don't be upset or concerned. Only about 30 to 40 percent of people using this technique get anything purpose-related the first time they try. That is why we have designed the **7 Steps** program with repeated uses of each spiritual discipline.

And, the good news is this: Even if, on any given day, God decides not to talk to you about your purpose while in prayer, you cannot spend time with the Lord without being changed. Prayer is not about getting God to act, it is designed to change you. Prayer takes you into the very presence of the Lord where He can soften your heart, change your focus, and prepare you for what lies ahead. Prayer is always beneficial.

COINCIDENCE OR GOD'S VOICE?

Here are a few more thoughts and reminders about hearing the Lord's voice:

- Don't expect God to speak to you in an audible voice or complete sentences. You're looking for insights, words, thoughts, pictures, or feelings.
- Pay particular attention to those things that just seem to pop into your head or fly into your heart. They may seem like random occurrences but we want you to learn to think differently about things that "just seem to happen."
- Watch for "coincidences." The Lord works through natural means, not just the miraculous. Quite often He will use everyday people, circumstances, and events to speak, to make an impact, or to do what only He can do. That's why it's so important to record everything, even if it seems coincidental or inconsequential at the time.

COINCIDENCE OR DIVINE INTERVENTION?

One evening, as we were going through **7 Steps to Purpose** with a small group, people were sharing how the Lord was speaking to them through their prayers, dreams, and meditation. A woman we'll call Lynn began telling how God had prompted her during prayer to invite her boss to church. She really didn't want to do it because he had said "no" so many times before. But in obedience, she did as she felt she was being told. The sermon that night was on marriage and afterward her boss shared that he and his wife were struggling—and not only that—he wanted to meet with the pastor to learn more about trying to save his marriage. WOW!

Well, that is not all that happened! As Lynn was telling this story, it was heard by another woman in our group, who we'll call Susan. The reality for Susan was that she had left her husband and was soon to be divorced. In the weeks that followed, we learned that what "just happened to be shared that night" became a turning point for Susan's marriage. She subsequently heard the Lord say, "Go back home and restore your marriage." Susan and her husband have since sought counseling and their marriage is well on the way to being reconciled. WOW again!

So…was all of this just coincidence or was it God lining up people and circumstances as a way of speaking?

What Susan could have easily overlooked as a story that had no personal application, the Lord turned into a clear message and assignment for her life. How sweet of God to speak this way. He not only honored Lynn's first act of obedience, but turned it into an additional opportunity for Susan to hear and obey…all leading to the blessing of two saved marriages.

WOW God!!!

WRAPPING IT UP

How much time did you spend in **purposeful prayer** today?

Describe your experience:

Record what you learned about your identity, destiny, and assignment:

Devote yourselves to prayer, being watchful and thankful. Colossians 4:2

Day 3 | Can You Hear God Speaking?

MEDITATION

In today's busy world, we are all so distracted that we rarely take the time to stop, relax, and listen to the Lord. This next discipline is designed to help you slow down, take the Word of the Lord in Scripture, and allow you to fully digest, dwell, and understand its meaning. Through this process, you will open an extraordinary path for the Lord to communicate His will. You will have the opportunity to seek the Lord and stay with a passage of Scripture until you are enlightened with both spiritual understanding and life application.

delve deep into His Word

You will seek me and find me when you seek me with all your heart. Jeremiah 29:13

In today's culture, meditation has taken on lots of different meanings. Most often it is based on a "New Age" approach to finding inner peace rather than a desire to seek the Lord. That is not how we define meditation. The kind of meditation we will introduce focuses on immersing yourself in the Word of God and hearing what He wants to teach you.

But his delight is in the law of the Lord, and on his law he meditates day and night. Psalm 1:2

Meditating is also a way to have a prayerful conversation with the Lord, giving you the opportunity to delve deep into His Word and discover all He has to say to you through a single verse of Scripture. If you give this discipline the proper time and focus, the Lord can share a depth of meaning and powerful insight that can be found few other ways.

SPIRITUAL DISCIPLINE 2: MEDITATION

Instructions:

1. Pick a time when you are not rushed or stressed. Find a quiet place which is private, where you will not be disturbed.

2. Have a pen and a pad or recording device.

3. You may use the Scripture we recommend or any other verse that God has given you during your search for purpose.

4. Read the verse you have selected, fully and slowly. Start at the beginning of the verse and contemplate the meaning of each phrase and word couplet.

5. Have a conversation with the Lord. Ask questions like: "What are you

saying to me?" "What is the meaning of this phrase?" "How does this relate to my purpose?" Add any other questions that are meaningful to you. Go deep with God and ask Him for all that He wants to reveal through this Scripture.

6. Now go to each individual word in the verse and dwell on it. Ask questions like the ones described in the previous step. Savor the words in your mind and heart. Take time and allow the Holy Spirit to open your understanding and begin to speak to you.

7. As you meditate, let the Holy Spirit personalize the meaning just for you. Let the Lord show you the greater meaning and power in both the individual words and the entire verse.

8. When you sense the Lord revealing information, thoughts, feelings, or insights, jot them down. Do this immediately following your meditation or while you're meditating if it is not too disruptive.

FOR FUTURE REFERENCE: You will be prompted in the days ahead to continue using this discipline. There will be many opportunities to seek the Lord for answers through meditation. We recommend that you tab this page of instructions with a sticky note or bookmark so it is easy to come back to and review.

Now, take time to seek God in meditation as outlined above.

Today's recommended verse (or you may chose your own if you feel called to another Scripture related to purpose).

Jeremiah 33:3 Choose the version that resonates with you:	
King James Version	Call unto Me, and I will answer thee, and show thee great and mighty things, which thou knowest not.
Amplified Bible	Call to Me and I will answer you and show you great and mighty things, fenced in and hidden, which you do not know (do not distinguish and recognize, have knowledge of and understand).
New American Standard Bible	Call to Me and I will answer you, and I will tell you great and mighty things, which you do not know.
New International Version	Call to Me and I will answer you and tell you great and unsearchable things you do not know.

Record your findings in the "Wrapping It Up" section at the end of today's work.

As you recorded your findings for your first day of meditation, how did it go for you? If it did not go as well as you had hoped, remember that this is a journey. You will have other opportunities to meditate again, plus you'll learn three more spiritual disciplines. One may work better for some and another better for others. It may also be a question of the Lord's timing. He may choose to use one discipline at a particular time, then move on to another method later.

Relax and enjoy the process!

ANOTHER WAY TO MEDITATE

And perhaps another way to approach meditation might help. Our good friend and licensed *Identity and Destiny* coach Robert Leatherwood has taught us—and many of our clients—his approach to meditation. We call it "Daily Manna." Let us share an excerpt from a recent blog post (www.IdentityandDestiny.com/blog) where Pam describes her experience with this technique:

> "A dear friend shared his morning 'routine' with me. I am excited to say that my mornings with the Lord are now so awesome I can hardly wait to get up and go meet with Him. (And I have to tell you...I am not a morning person...so, this truly must be a work of God in my life!)
>
> It begins by getting up before daylight...finding a Scripture on which to meditate...writing the verse on a sticky note to carry in the palm of my hand...and going out for an hour of walking, running, biking...whatever.
>
> I am a walker...I start with my favorite praise and worship on my iPod...then I remove the ear buds...and simply listen. I love hearing the birds and the sounds of the day awakening around me. I will often gaze toward heaven and simply soak up God's beautiful creation! Then, I begin to pray. I take my chosen Scripture apart—word by word—and ask the Lord (out loud) what He wants to show me. I chew on it...I search for the depths of its truth and meaning for my life. **Prayer has turned into a conversation with God...deep...real...meaningful!!!**
>
> There are days when I feel the joy of the Lord as I have never known it. I feel as if God is saying, 'Thank you for coming out here and spending time with Me...thank you for asking Me about My Word...thank you for seeking My wisdom.'
>
> My best days are the ones when I am able to start with this 'feast on the Word of God.' It is time spent seeking the Lord with all my heart, mind, and strength. It is about hiding God's Word in my heart. I call it my **Manna for the Day**."

A client also recently emailed us about his experience using this technique:

> "I just wanted to let you know that I incorporated Robert's practice of walking and meditating on a verse this morning. I did not know what verse to use, but the Holy Spirit gave my wife Psalm 61:5... ***"For you have heard my vows, O God; you have given me the heritage of those who fear your name."*** WOW! Cathy, the Holy Spirit, and I had the most awesome walk/conversation dissecting this verse. What a great idea. I will be doing it every morning."

GOD WILL MEET YOU

When you meditate, you can vary your method to keep the experience fresh and enjoyable. But know this: No matter what time of day or how you choose to work with this discipline, when you meditate on Scripture, the Lord will meet you right where you are. He will reveal the message you need to hear and the meaning you are capable of understanding. The Word of the Lord is alive and active. It is continually able to give new insight and instruction every time you read and meditate on it.

For the word of God is living and active. Sharper than any double-edged sword, it penetrates even to dividing soul and spirit, joints and marrow; it judges the thoughts and attitudes of the heart. Hebrews 4:12

WRAPPING IT UP

Remember: the spiritual disciplines are to be cumulative.

Continue with **purposeful prayer**, asking the Lord about your identity, destiny, and assignment as instructed on Day 2 of Step 5. Jot down His answers here.

Record what you have learned through today's **meditation.** Don't forget: the Lord may not speak in complete sentences. You're looking for thoughts, feelings, pictures, and places. Don't worry about whether it makes sense; it will all come together as you create the mosaic of your identity and destiny.

Whatever is true, whatever is noble, whatever is right, whatever is pure, whatever is lovely, whatever is admirable—if anything is excellent or praiseworthy—think about such things. Philippians 4:8

Day 4 | *Can You Hear God Speaking?*

DREAMS

Henry and Richard Blackaby's book, *Hearing God's Voice*, cites 24 ways that the Lord spoke to His people in the Old Testament and 16 ways that He spoke in the New Testament. Richard Mull, our good friend and founder of Operation Light Force (www.operationlightforce.com), says the list is far longer. His research shows that God spoke 22 different ways in the book of Acts alone.

the Lord did indeed speak

The important point is that the Lord did indeed speak—uniquely, specifically, and directly. And one of the ways He chose to speak in both the Old and New Testaments was dreams. For example, visit the details of Joseph in Genesis 40 and the Magi in Matthew 2.

Experts trained in dream analysis and interpretation say that dreams are a direct means of access to the unconscious mind as well as the soul. And even though there are those who question whether the Lord still speaks through dreams, our personal experience—and the experience of many clients—confirms that God is still actively communicating this way.

As you practice this exercise, know that statistically only a small percentage of people report getting clear insight or communication from dreams. However, we are confident that it can still be a worthwhile part of your purpose pursuit.

If you don't seem to be getting anything, don't worry. Try it every night for the next few weeks and again from time to time as you learn to live on purpose. Also, be mindful as you go forward that the Lord may speak when you haven't focused on asking for a dream. Get in the habit of recording anything that seems to stick with you the next day. If God knows you are truly seeking Him and that you are willing to follow His plan for your life, He will make that known to you in His perfect timing. And He might just use a dream to help reveal it.

Some indications that dreams may be spiritual:

- You actually remember the dream the next morning.
- You get an immediate (next few days) interpretation or confirmation.
- You have a dream that is persistent or recurring.

It is important to pay attention to what happens next.

- Often the Lord plants a seed in your dreams, and then He will bring circumstances, other people, events, or a particular Scripture across your path to help your dream make sense. He will expand the meaning and may even show you what it is all about.

PAM'S DREAM AND WHAT HAPPENED NEXT

"June 13, 2001, I awoke early from an odd but interesting dream:

In my dream I was making homemade yeast bread with my grandmother just like we did when I was a child. The odd thing was that the yeast had become so aggressive that the dough just kept multiplying. My 14–year-old daughter was there helping and I was busy handing her big sections of the dough, asking her to help as my grandmother and I tried to keep up with the kneading process.

As I got dressed that morning, I passed it off as one of those silly things that only happens in dreams.

Later that day, as I was driving to a friend's house, I heard a pastor on the radio talking about how the Bible often refers to yeast as sin. He said it takes only a little to "infect" the whole batch of dough. His words hit me like a ton of bricks. I thought about my dream and handing the dough to my young daughter—dough that was infected with sin. I knew, right then and there, my dream the night before was not just something silly, but a message from the Lord about my life.

In the six months prior I had begun trying to get to know God through a neighborhood Bible study. I believed in God, but had never really spent any time in Scripture. I had not yet surrendered my life to Christ. I was still trying to do life my way by trying to make it happen in my own power and strength. But, in all honesty, it wasn't going so well. In the eyes of the world, I was a great success. But with divorce and a broken home in my past, I knew that the way I was living my life was not God's best. And, in my heart, I knew my children deserved so much better.

On that day, the Lord used my dream to show me how much I needed Him. He revealed Himself, not just as God, but as my Savior. He let me know that if I would turn my life over to Him, then He would fill that empty place in my soul that nothing else had ever been able to fill. He let me know that, through his Son, Jesus Christ, I could have the forgiveness, the life, the hope, and the peace that I had wanted here on earth–PLUS eternity with Him in Heaven."

For Pam, June 13, 2001 was not just another day that started with a random dream. It was the beginning of how the Lord would choose to speak to her and then line up subsequent circumstances that would help her dream make sense. And ultimately, it led to her day of salvation.

Remember: the Lord may use your dreams to plant a thought that only becomes clear when something else happens. He may speak in ways that can only be understood when you pay attention to what happens next and apply it to the overall landscape of your life.

Dreams can also be an important part of validating your identity, destiny, or assignment as you near completion of the **7 Steps to Purpose**. Incorporating the discipline in your daily prayer life now may bring wonderful returns.

Learn to listen to your dreams, have fun, and enjoy this part of the journey.

SPIRITUAL DISCIPLINE 3: DREAMS

Instructions:

1. Before you go to sleep, make sure your **7 Steps** workbook and a pen are handy, on your bedside table or on the vanity in your bathroom. (You will need to quickly record your dreams upon waking, even in the middle of the night. Important details that are not immediately recorded can be quickly forgotten.)

2. As you prepare to go to bed, begin by calming yourself and setting aside the stress of the day. Seek the Lord in prayer and faith. Let Him know that you are ready and willing to know the purpose that He has for you.

3. Pray and ask the Lord to give you a dream specific to your purpose. Start one evening with a request for dreams about your identity. Then on following evenings ask about your destiny and then your assignment. Ask Him to be clear and direct. Ask that He would give you perfect recall upon waking. Pray for wisdom and discernment, to know what is purpose-related and what is not.

4. Upon waking, don't worry about whether it all makes sense. Just record anything that you remember, including words, pictures, or feelings.

5. Just capture the information. This will be one more set of clues or pointers that will be assessed in the context of all the work you do in your purpose pursuit.

FOR FUTURE REFERENCE: You will be prompted in the days ahead to continue using this discipline. There will be many opportunities to seek the Lord for answers through dreams. We recommend that you tab this page of instructions with a sticky note or bookmark so it is easy to come back to and review.

Take time tonight to pray for purpose-related dreams as outlined above and record your findings in the "Wrapping It Up" section at the end of today's work.

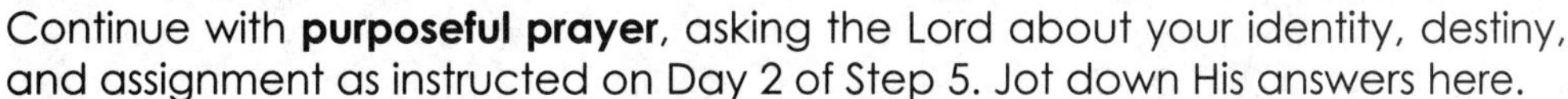

WRAPPING IT UP

BE ENCOURAGED: the spiritual disciplines are cumulative, and some people may have better results with one than another.

Continue with **purposeful prayer**, asking the Lord about your identity, destiny, and assignment as instructed on Day 2 of Step 5. Jot down His answers here.

Continue with **meditation** as instructed on Day 3 of Step 5. Use the recommended verse below or a verse of your choosing.

Proverbs 3:5-6 Choose the version that resonates with you:	
King James Version	Trust in the LORD with all your heart, and lean not on your own understanding; In all your ways acknowledge Him, and He shall direct your paths.
Amplified Bible	Lean on, trust in, and be confident in the Lord with all your heart and mind and do not rely on your own insight or understanding. In all your ways know, recognize, and acknowledge Him, and He will direct and make straight and plain your paths.
New American Standard Bible	Trust in the LORD with all your heart and do not lean on your own understanding. In all your ways acknowledge Him, and He will make your paths straight.
New International Version	Trust in the LORD with all your heart and lean not on your own understanding; In all your ways acknowledge him, and he will make your paths straight.

Record what you have learned through today's **meditation.** Don't forget: the Lord isn't likely to speak in complete sentences. You're looking for thoughts, feelings, pictures, and places. Don't worry about whether it makes sense; it will all come together as you create the mosaic of your identity and destiny.

Capture anything that you remember from last night's **dreams**, including words, pictures, or feelings.

During the night the mystery was revealed to Daniel in a vision. Then Daniel praised the God of heaven and said...He gives wisdom to the wise and knowledge to the discerning, He reveals deep and hidden things; he knows what lies in darkness and light dwells with him. Daniel 2:19; 21-22

Day 5 | *Can You Hear God Speaking?*

LET'S REVIEW AND REMEMBER

Another week comes to a close. Congratulations again!

As you go about life with all your daily deadlines and emergencies, we hope you are finding time to spend with the Lord and learning to enjoy the three spiritual disciplines introduced this week.

We also want to acknowledge the tremendous amount of ground you've covered in the past six weeks, and tell you we know it can sometimes be a bit overwhelming.

Let's slow down and take a look back to remember why you started this process.

What was your primary goal as you started **7 Steps to Purpose**?

Ultimately, it is to discover your God-given purpose!

Once you know your purpose, you will:

- Gain deep self-awareness and the freedom to love yourself just the way the Lord created you.
- Experience the tangible day-to-day benefits of a life lived on purpose, including clarity, confidence, energy, and enthusiasm.
- Deepen your relationship and intimacy with the Lord as you seek His will and fulfill the plan He has for your life.

STAY THE COURSE

We also want you to know, if you find yourself feeling anxious and uncertain, you are NOT alone! Almost everyone who completes the **7 Steps to Purpose** faces some level of frustration as they finish Step 4 and move into the Phase III work that focuses on communicating directly with the Lord.

As you enter this final phase, we encourage you to simply stay the course and ask the Lord for help when you feel yourself wavering. The disciplines you are learning and the time you are spending with the Lord are meant to be habits of a lifetime so don't be too hard on yourself if you don't get it perfect the first few weeks. Just take it one day at a time, do the best you can, and commit to finishing strong.

We promise, it will be worth it!

the power to say "NO"

Thankfully, knowing your God-given purpose can help alleviate an enormous amount of your stress. You'll have a plumb line for your life, and an internal compass for making wise, God-directed decisions. In a world of too many choices and too much to do, it is critical to have a way of setting priorities and eliminating things that don't line up with God's purpose.

As *Identity and Destiny* licensee Robert Leatherwood said when he first completed the program: "I now have a power that very few people have. I have the power to say NO, because my YES is so big!"

Whoa! Stop and meditate on that for a moment.

Having that kind of power should be reason enough to find, know, and live your God-given purpose! Now, let's finish Step 5 using the three spiritual disciplines as outlined in today's "Wrapping It Up!"

WRAPPING IT UP

Remember: the spiritual disciplines are to be cumulative.

Continue with **purposeful prayer**, asking the Lord about your identity, destiny, and assignment as instructed on Day 2 of Step 5. Jot down His answers here.

Continue with **meditation** as instructed on Day 3 of Step 5. Use the recommended verse below or a verse of your choosing.

Ephesians 2:10 Choose the version that resonates with you:	
King James Version	For we are his workmanship, created in Christ Jesus unto good works, which God hath before ordained that we should walk in them.
Amplified Bible	For we are God's [own] handiwork (His workmanship), recreated in Christ Jesus, [born anew] that we may do those good works which God predestined (planned beforehand) for us [taking paths which He prepared ahead of time], that we should walk in them [living the good life which He prearranged and made ready for us to live].
New American Standard Bible	For we are His workmanship, created in Christ Jesus for good works, which God prepared beforehand so that we would walk in them.
New International Version	For we are God's workmanship, created in Christ Jesus to do good works, which God prepared in advance for us to do.

Record what you have learned through today's **meditation**.

Continue asking the Lord for **dreams** about your identity, destiny, and purpose as instructed on Day 4 of Step 5. Capture anything you remember, including words, pictures, or feelings.

Humble yourselves, therefore, under God's almighty hand, that he may lift you up in due time. Cast all you anxiety on him because he cares for you. 1 Peter 5:6-7

Review | *Can You Hear God Speaking?*

KEY POINTS TO REMEMBER!

- The Prayer of Commitment: Your agreement with the Lord to abandon self-will and go forward in the plan He has for your life.
- God speaks to his people and you can learn to hear His voice!
- Coincidences are the Lord choosing to remain anonymous. But His divine hand of intervention is ever-present if you learn to recognize it.
- You have now learned how to listen with your heart and emotions.
- You've learned how to use a "Crystal Box" to keep the critical, skeptical, and judgmental parts of your brain out of the way as you listen for the Lord's voice.
- Your relationship with the Lord is like the ones you share with your very best friends. It requires spending time together to build real intimacy.
- Purposeful prayer, meditation, and dreams are all disciplines that open your heart and soul to God and allow Him to clearly speak.
- There is power in knowing your purpose: the power to say "NO" because your "YES" is so big!

My Big "Aha"
What was the most dramatic or important thing you learned this week?

Capture It!
Go back through your notes and record the most important words, phrases, pictures, feelings, concepts, and key thoughts that have come from your week's work.

God's Word
Identify the Scripture that impacted you most deeply this week and journal your thoughts in the following format:

Write out the Scripture:

Identify its **message** to you:

How can you **apply** that to your life?

Write a **prayer** back to God about this Scripture. Thank Him, ask for help, or just talk it through, whatever feels right.

Personal Notes, Thoughts, and Journaling

STEP 6 | WEEK SEVEN

Can You "Be Still" and Listen?

GUIDED LISTENING PRAYER

DIALOGUE JOURNALING

Day 1 | Can You "Be Still" and Listen?

a very special week

WELCOME TO STEP 6!

In Step 6, you will continue your quest to hear God's voice and learn your purpose. You will be encouraged to use the spiritual disciplines from last week, plus two new ones we will add to your repertoire. But, please don't be overwhelmed by that thought. We won't be asking you to do all five disciplines each day.

Other than a couple days of meditation that will be assigned, you are at liberty to use last week's disciplines when, and if, you choose. However, we want your primary focus this week to be the two new disciplines we will introduce.

THE BEST WEEK OF ALL

Clients have repeatedly told us Step 6 is the most exciting of them all! They tell us guided listening prayer and dialogue journaling are the disciplines that help them finally learn to genuinely "be still" and listen.

With rare exception, guided listening prayer and dialogue journaling bring the greatest level of results and insight. They open communication with the Lord in ways that allow the "conversation" to really flow. We're not sure if it's the techniques themselves that are at the heart of these results or the cumulative impact of everything you've done to this point. But, whatever it is, rest assured you are in for a very special week with the Lord!

We will begin Step 6 by teaching our fourth spiritual discipline, guided listening prayer. But, before we get into the detailed instructions for this assignment, let's spend a little more time talking about prayer and then the specifics of guided listening prayer in particular.

PRAYER: A REGULAR PRACTICE?

Over the years, surveys reveal that most of our clients pray but, when asked, they admit they don't pray often or consistently. Many also tell us they don't feel they really know how to pray.

If this is true for you, let us direct you to some resources on our website's recommended reading list at www.IdentityandDestiny.com. Some of our personal favorites are:

- *Praying God's Word* by Beth Moore
- *The Power of Simple Prayer* by Joyce Meyer
- *Too Busy Not to Pray* by Bill Hybels

Or maybe you spend regular time in prayer but find it's rather brief and perhaps a bit casual. You may pray but still not have the rich and meaningful communication with the Lord that you desire.

Don't get us wrong, God understands the need for emergency prayers—the quick spur-of-the-moment kind that show your raw, transparent need—but we suggest that should not be the norm. If you are always running to God distracted, in a hurry, and with a specific need in mind, you will never get to the deepest level of prayer and intimacy.

God wants to speak to you and He wants to share ***great and unsearchable things you do not know. Jeremiah 33:3***

But you must give Him your time and attention. You must make the effort to spend time with Him on a regular basis.

PRIVILEDGE VERSES OBLIGATION

Throughout the Old Testament, God details a whole host of sacrifices and rituals required to enter His presence. Fortunately, through Christ, we now have the opportunity to enjoy direct access to God in prayer. Scripture actually says we can come boldly before the throne of God. Think of that! How awesome that you can go directly to God with your worship, confession, requests, and thanksgiving!

Let us then approach the throne of grace with confidence, so that we may receive mercy and find grace to help us in our time of need. Hebrews 4:16

If you are able to think of prayer as a privileged opportunity rather than a daily obligation, you might be more likely to enjoy it. You might, if you do not already, begin to treasure this precious gift you have been given.

PRAYER IS ALL ABOUT RELATIONSHIP

As a final thought before you begin today's exercise, let us remind you of something which at first may seem confusing:

Fear of the Lord is the beginning of all wisdom. Psalm 111:10

The kind of fear the Psalm is talking about is not being scared to death. It's about respect. In the context of prayer, it means approaching your Creator in a manner befitting His holiness. We would suggest this means not always coming before Him distracted, harried, and rushed. It means spending time getting mentally and emotionally prepared for honest, loving, and respectful dialogue.

Isn't that the least we should do to honor Him?

Regardless of how you come before Him, more than anything else God wants an intimate, love relationship with each and every one of you. And there's no better way to do that than getting together with Him on a regular basis. That's what prayer is all about. He waits patiently for you each day. He wants you to slow down long enough to meet with Him.

Think again of someone you are very close to. Do you miss them when you haven't talked for awhile? Do you get to the point where you long to hear their voice? The good news is this: Just one phone call or conversation and communication with your friend is restored. Soon your relationship can be headed back toward intimacy.

Your relationship with God is no different. Don't keep Him waiting any longer. Go to Him now and make the commitment to make prayer part of each and every day.

GOD WANTS YOU TO LISTEN

you'll know when God speaks

Now, as we turn to this week's first new discipline of guided listening prayer, we want you to begin thinking of prayer as a two-way conversation between you and God—with God doing most of the talking. Rather than the more typical one-way monologue where you do most of the talking, we want you to focus on "being still" and listening.

To help you get started, we want to share some thoughts from the best resource we have ever found on the practice of listening prayer. It is Mary Geegh's booklet *God Guides*. Mary was a missionary in India who learned to actively engage God in prayer by listening. In her book, she journals many amazing experiences along with the testimony of thousands of changed lives. Although this little book is only a brief 60 pages, it is profoundly life-altering for many people!

Mary shares about her journey to learn the practice of listening prayer:

> "Be quiet and God's whisper will come to you without fail...pure, honest, loving and unselfish. You'll know it when God speaks. You will hear it with your heart not just your mind."

Mary also states:

> "When man listens, God speaks;
> When man obeys, God acts;
> When God acts, men change;
> When men change, nations change."

Don Barefoot is president of the C12 Group (www.c12group.com), an organization dedicated to CEO's and business owners who are building their businesses for a greater purpose. He writes about Geegh's approach to listening prayer:

> "We all do not hear in the same way. Some experience a tweaked conscience or impression in their Spirit. Others receive a picture, a vision or hear a clear answer. Still others are directed to a specific Bible verse or trustworthy counselor. In any case, listening prayer helps us discover His plans for us and enables us to listen and obey."

Finally, Ron Morin, president of Pray America, writes in his introduction to Mary's book:

> "Our prayer for you is that you will be exhorted through this book to explore "listening prayer" as a means to a living and vibrant faith that stretches your understanding of God and His wonderful plan for you. Listen...Obey. It is truly that simple."

DIVE DEEPER

At the time of this writing, Mary Geegh's book *God Guides* is available for $4.00 per copy at www.prayamerica.org or contact:

Pray America
P.O. Box 14070
Lansing MI 48901-4070
(517) 622-1085

GUIDED LISTENING PRAYER

To start this exercise, begin by going to the Resource section of our website at www.IdentityandDestiny.com. Go to Chapter 7 - Step 6 to access and listen to the Guided Listening Prayer audio session. (You can also use the following link to go directly to the section of the site that houses the Guided Listening Prayer: http://www.IdentityandDestiny.com/guided-listening-prayer.php)

In this session, Tom will be your guide as you listen to soft music designed to quiet your mind and open your spirit. It is with much gratitude, we thank Jacob Hamby who wrote and produced the inspired music that will accompany you through your Guided Listening Prayer sessions.

Instructions:

1. Pick a time when you are not rushed or stressed. Find a quiet place that is private and where you will not be disturbed.

2. Open your workbook and have a pen so you can take notes during or immediately after this exercise.

3. Unlike some prayer disciplines, a suitable posture for this exercise is lying down or sitting in a high-back chair where you can rest your head.

4. Prepare yourself physically by getting comfortable and taking a few slow, deep, relaxing breaths.

5. Prepare yourself mentally by shutting out the world and its stresses. Relax in the arms of the Lord. Tell Him how you want to seek His will and obey what you hear. Tell Him again that you are ready and willing to surrender. Tell Him how excited you are to find, know, and live the purpose He has for your life.

6. Realize the Lord speaks in many ways. It could be a feeling, a thought, a word, a phrase that might come into your mind, or even a picture; all are possibilities.

As Henry Blackaby says:

> "Just as we are forced to listen carefully when someone speaks softly, so by God speaking to us in many ways, we are forced to pay close attention to what He is communicating. Keep your heart open to all the ways God wants to communicate with you."

FOR FUTURE REFERENCE: You will be prompted in the days ahead to continue using this discipline. There will be several opportunities for you to seek God for answers through guided listening prayer as you finish the **7 Steps to Purpose**. We also hope that you will continue to use this discipline for years to come. We recommend that you tab this page of instructions with a sticky note or bookmark so it is easy to come back to and review.

Special Note: The first time you listen to the guided listening prayer, you will want to go through the full introduction. But once you become familiar with the process, you may want to skip the instructions and get started more quickly. We have created a slightly shorter version of the audio so you can skip the introductory section and make repeated use more convenient. There are instructions with the download at www.IdentityandDestiny.com on how to access the "no intro" version of guided listening prayer.

Now, take time to seek God through guided listening prayer as outlined above. Then, record your findings in the "Wrapping It Up" section at the end of today's work.

FAMILIARITY BRINGS SUCCESS

If you find that this first attempt at guided listening prayer found you a little distracted or confused, don't be concerned. It is common to feel a bit uncertain as you become comfortable with the process and the content.

The second time you listen will be more effective because of your familiarly with the process. Then, listening a third time and beyond will have greater and greater impact. Give yourself time to become familiar with the technology, and more importantly, remember it takes time to learn to slow down and really listen.

Whatever you do, don't give up on this discipline! There is much to be gained through guided listening prayer.

WRAPPING IT UP

The only spiritual discipline you will be asked to work on today is guided listening prayer. Hopefully you have done the exercise as outlined above and are ready to record your findings. If not, please do so now.

Make note here of the thoughts, feelings, words, pictures, or anything else you received as you did your first day of **guided listening prayer:**

We ask God to give you complete understanding of what he wants to do in your lives; and we ask him to make you wise with spiritual wisdom. Colossians 1:9

Day 2 | Can You "Be Still" and Listen?

HEARING GOD'S VOICE:

As we start Day 2, let us take a quick inventory.

Are the four spiritual disciplines you've learned beginning to produce good results? Are you getting communication from the Lord about your purpose? If so, CONGRATULATIONS! Please carry on, continue to seek God for revelation, and don't forget to take time to thank Him along the way.

God has something good in store

If this isn't the case, you may be among those who get to this point and still feel stuck. You may find yourself thinking, *I'm just not getting anything of value*. If so, we want to encourage you to keep working the disciplines and trust that God has something good in store if you persevere.

Blessed is the man who perseveres under trial, because when he has stood the test, he will receive the crown of life that God has promised to those who love him. James 1:12

We also want to spend some time today asking you to consider a few final obstacles that could be in the way:

First, could it be that God just isn't ready to speak yet?

We don't believe that God plays games when it comes to finding your purpose. But, He may be using silence as a way to get you to continue seeking in faith. He may be using this time to build trust and relationship that can be sustained without signs and miracles, those assurances we so often clamor for. Rather than becoming frustrated, you might want to consider this a deep and intimate way of God refining and building your maturity for what lies ahead.

Why not simply relax and enjoy your time with Him? In faith, continue using the techniques we are teaching and learn to wait. Yes, that can be one of the hardest things you will ever learn to do in your relationship with God, yet it is one of the most important! As our pastor Matthew Hartsfield says: "We live in a microwave world and have a crockpot God."

Let all that I am wait quietly before God, for my hope is in him. Psalm 62:5

Do you feel like God may be teaching you to wait? How could you begin to approach this differently?

Second, is it time to take a look at yourself and your relationship with others? Is there reconciliation you need to pursue with a spouse, family member, friend, or co-worker? Is there something you know God wants you to do, but you are resisting?

Silence with regard to your purpose may be God saying, "Go deal with these things first. Then we can talk about where we go from here."
Read the following Scriptures. See who and what God brings to mind:

Why do you look at the speck of sawdust in your brother's eye and pay no attention to the plank in your own eye? First take the plank out of your own eye. Matthew 7:3, 5

Therefore, if you are offering your gift at the altar and there remember that your brother has something against you; leave your gift there in front of the altar. First go and be reconciled to your brother; then come and offer your gift to me. Matthew 5:23-24

Do not repay anyone evil for evil. Be careful to do what is right in the eyes of everybody. If it is possible, as far as it depends on you, live at peace with everyone. Romans 12:17-18

- Is there "work" God wants you to do first?
- Is there something you know God wants you to change, but you still haven't been obedient?
- Is there a judgmental spirit in you toward others?
- Is there confession needed between you and God?
- Are there amends needed between you and others?
- Are there areas of forgiveness needed?
- Is there reconciliation or restoration needed?

Will you go to God now and begin this work?

If there are other issues that you need to resolve, will you begin that process now?

Finally, if you are not hearing from God, we have already discussed the possibility that sin may be blocking His voice. Step 4 has tools you may want to go back and revisit, but according to Scripture, the bottom line is this: Repent and return to God**.** And when you do, He stands ready to forgive and restore relationship!

If we confess our sins, he is faithful and just and will forgive our sins and purify us from all unrighteousness. 1 John 1:9

But, what we want to talk about today is not "returning" to the Lord, but "turning" to Him, perhaps for the very first time. If you are like Pam in the story she shared about her dream, you may know God and you may even know the story of Jesus dying on the cross for your sins. Even if you know and believe that, you may still have only an intellectual understating of God. You may have it figured out in your head but never gotten it down into your heart.

Having an intimate and personal relationship with God goes beyond intellectual understanding and agreement—it requires a heartfelt commitment to turn your life and your will over to God. You need to be able to accept your need for a Savior and believe that Christ is the only one who can satisfy that need. It is a love relationship with God through His Son, Jesus Christ, that produces the kind of genuine shift in attitude and perspective that is required.

Do you have a heartfelt relationship with God through His Son, Jesus Christ? Let's take a look at some basic truths as found in Scripture to help you answer this eternally important question:

turn your will over to God

There is no one who is righteous. (Romans 3:10)

We have all sinned and fall short. (Romans 3:23)

Sin brings death and eternal separation from God. (Romans 6:23)

God loves you and wants to save you. (Romans 5:8)

Jesus is the way to be reconciled to God. (John 14:6)

It is by faith that you can have this kind of relationship. (Ephesians 2:8-9)

Confess and believe that Jesus is Lord. (Romans 10:9-10)

When you believe you are "born again." (John 3:1-8)

All who call on the name of the Lord will be saved. (Romans 10:13)

Jesus stands at the door of your heart and knocks. (Revelation 3:20)

Will you invite Him into your heart? Is today the day you will invite Jesus into your life and allow him to be your Lord and Savior?

If you mean business, the following prayer shows how you can do that now:

> **Dear Jesus,**
>
> **Today, I confess that I'm a sinner in need of a savior, and I ask for Your love, mercy, grace, and forgiveness. Thank You for dying on the cross, forgiving my sins, and giving me eternal life. Please come into my heart and my life. Help me be all You want me to be. Today, I surrender my life and my will to You. I want You to be the one I call Lord and Savior from this day forward.**
>
> **Amen.**

If this reflects the desire of your heart, please pray this prayer to Jesus now.

And just as we did when you prayed the Prayer of Commitment in Step 5, please sign and date the space below as a memorial of the day of your salvation. Praise God!

Signature____________________________________ Date________________

NEED MORE ANSWERS?

If you're not sure you are ready to pray this prayer of salvation, have unanswered questions, or want more information, please spend some time with your pastor or spiritual mentor, or visit the following websites and learn more about what it means to have a personal relationship with Jesus Christ:

Campus Crusade for Christ International at www.ccci.org

Billy Graham Evangelistic Association at www.billygraham.org

We also highly recommend that you take just a few minutes and watch Pastor Matthew Hartsfield's video. It is one of the clearest and most helpful explanations about entering a personal relationship with Christ we have ever seen. Go to www.IdentityandDestiny.com and click on the Resources tab.

CONCLUSION

Clearing the way to hear God's voice and truly being in relationship with Him is at the heart of the **7 Steps to Purpose.**

First, you must know God intimately and personally. Then, you will have His Holy Spirit dwelling in you to guide you in the search for purpose. The Bible says that without the power of the Holy Spirit, things of God can seem like foolishness. They cannot be understood intellectually. They must be understood spiritually.

But the Counselor, the Holy Spirit, whom the Father will send in my name, will teach you all things. John 14:26

But people who aren't spiritual can't receive these truths from God's Spirit. It all sounds foolish to them and they can't understand it, for only those who are spiritual can understand what the Spirit means. 1 Corinthians 2:14

The Lord wants you to know Him and learn to hear His unmistakable voice. When that happens, it will change your life forever!

DIVE DEEPER

This is another spot in the **7 Steps to Purpose** where a trained coach may help optimize your experience. We encourage you to visit www.IdentityandDestiny.com and learn more about the coaches who have completed our certified training programs and the "laser coaching" sessions we've created to target specific concerns without requiring a long-term commitment. Custom-designed services provide the help, support, and encouragement you need.

WRAPPING IT UP

Let's finish today with two of our spiritual disciplines: meditation and guided listening prayer.

Continue with **meditation** as instructed on Day 3 of Step 5. Use the recommended verse below or a verse of your choosing.

Jeremiah 29:11 Choose the version that resonates with you:	
King James Version	For I know the thoughts that I think toward you, saith the LORD, thoughts of peace, and not of evil, to give you an expected end.
Amplified Bible	For I know the thoughts and plans that I have for you, says the Lord, thoughts and plans for welfare and peace and not for evil, to give you hope in your final outcome.
New American Standard Bible	For I know the plans that I have for you, declares the LORD, plans for welfare and not for calamity to give you a future and a hope.
New International Version	For I know the plans I have for you, declares the LORD, plans to prosper you and not to harm you, plans to give you hope and a future.

Jot down what you have learned through today's **meditation.** Don't forget, the Lord may not speak in complete sentences. You're looking for thoughts, feelings, pictures, and places.

Now, take time to seek the Lord through **guided listening prayer** as outlined on Day 1 of Step 6. Then, record your experience below. Capture everything that God reveals—no editing yet—just collect what He brings to mind as you listen for His voice.

Finally, if you have received any **other messages, images, or information** from the Lord that go beyond today's meditation and guided listening prayer, please make a note of them here. It could be from your personal time in prayer, your dreams, while reading Scripture, something someone has said, or a word directly from God during the course of your day.

Day 3 | Can You "Be Still" and Listen?

JOURNALING WITH GOD

Today we are going to jump right into the fifth, and final, spiritual discipline. In this exercise, you are going to journal with the Lord. We call it dialogue journaling.

If you're already in the habit of journaling or you regularly chronicle your life with posts on sites like Twitter and Facebook, you are sure to have a lot of fun with today's exercise. Many participants tell us this exercise brings the greatest level of breakthrough—once they allow themselves to engage without reservation!

Like all the other disciplines detailed in the **7 Steps to Purpose**, you must suspend skepticism and judgment to give the Lord control of your pen as you write the questions and answers during dialogue journaling. But, once you've mastered the technique, you'll be able to look back at what you have written and know the answers did not come from you. You will know that the Lord clearly directed the pen to write what ended up on your paper.

Before you start, you will definitely want to pull out your "Crystal Box" and keep the "three amigos" well under control as you work through this exercise. They can come out later and help you confirm what the Lord is telling you, but they need to stay out of the way while you're doing this work.

DIALOGUE JOURNALING

Instructions:
Dialogue journaling can be an extremely effective way to validate insights you receive in other prayer disciplines. Through pen, paper and the time you will spend journaling, this discipline is one more highly effective way to hear God speak directly to you. This exercise will start just as you did with the guided listening prayer and meditation exercises, but then we'll add a new twist:

1. Find a quiet place to get away from the distractions of your day. Be ready with pen and paper. A space is provided in the "Wrapping It Up" section to capture the essence of what you learn in your dialogue journaling, but for the exercise itself, we recommend a separate note pad or journal. If you and the Lord really get going, you could have several pages of notes by the time you are finished with any given session.

2. BE SURE to put the "three amigos" of skepticism, judgment, and criticism in the Crystal Box and shut them away for the duration of this exercise. If you need help remembering this exercise, refer back to Day 1 of Step 5.

3. Relax and take a few deep breaths.

4. Slowly read the following Scripture verses several times as you get into the proper mental state.

   Call me and I will answer you, and tell you great and unsearchable things you do not know. Jeremiah 33:3

   For I know the plans I have for you, declares the LORD, plans to prosper you and not to harm you, plans to give you hope and a future. Then you will call upon me and come and pray to me, and I will listen to you. You will seek me and find me when you seek me with all your heart. Jeremiah 29:11-13

5. Ask the Lord to speak with you in your journaling.

6. Write a question, like the ones suggested below, asking the Lord for information about your identity. Ask just as though you were speaking to Him. Ask any question you like and stay neutral, non-judgmental, and open to the answers. Just go with the flow.

7. Similarly, write down the answer you receive in your own mind. Don't worry if you are "making it up" or not. Again, just go with the flow.

8. Pretend you're writing a screen play. To help you get the idea, the following is one of Tom's dialogue journaling sessions. He had already received purpose information through the other disciplines, so this was part of his confirmation as well as continued seeking.

   Tom: Lord, will You speak to me this morning?

   The Lord: Of course, I'm always with you.

   Tom: What is the identity You created for me?

   The Lord: I have already given you all I have for now.

   Tom: What can You tell me about my destiny?

   The Lord: You've already got that too.

   Tom: What is my assignment?

   The Lord: Focus on Christians, build a business—I will direct you.

   Tom: Will You help me work on the details of my destiny?

   The Lord: Yes.

   Tom: For whom is this intended?

The Lord: All people, but start with the Christian community.

Tom: In what emotional or mental state is a person when they need help finding their destiny and purpose?

The Lord: Questioning, curious, transitioning, tumultuous.

Tom: What are the steps?

The Lord: Four parts—they will come together.

Tom: What's my impact to be? What effect does my destiny produce?

The Lord: Love and honor others, Make them feel good about themselves. Encouragement, improved self-image, focus.

Tom: Am I a messenger?

The Lord: Yes.

Tom: What is my message?

The Lord: You are okay! I made you to be who you are—now run with it!!!

Tom: Lord, thank You for all You have done for me in my life… and for being with me today.

FOR FUTURE REFERENCE: You will be prompted in the days ahead to continue using this discipline. There will be several opportunities for you to seek the Lord for answers through dialogue journaling as you finish the **7 Steps** program. We also hope that you will continue to use this discipline for years to come. We recommend that you tab this page of instructions with a sticky note or bookmark so it is easy to come back to and review.

Questions you might ask…
As you develop your list of questions for dialogue journaling, think about asking in terms of identity, destiny, and assignment. Then, once the conversation is underway, be sure to ask additional questions for greater understanding and detail.

Also ask the Lord for His **E-S-V:** Elaboration, Specification, and Validation.

Questions for Identity:

- What one word describes who I am at my very core?
- Who am I?
- What am I uniquely designed to be in this world?

- Is there any experience from my past that has uniquely designed me to be who I am?
- How do I recognize and use that formative experience?
- Who do You say I am, Lord?
- What possibilities have You placed within me?

Questions for Destiny:

- What is my destiny?
- Why am I here?
- What is the work that You and Your Holy Spirit want to do through me?
- What is it You created me to do?
- Where am I to exercise my destiny?
- For what group or individuals is it intended?
- How will I know who, when, and where?
- What impact will my destiny have?

Is this really God?

Questions for Assignment:

- What assignment/task do You have for me?
- Who am I to help?
- What message am I to deliver?
- How do I perform this assignment?
- How do I get started?
- How can I best serve You?

Now, take time to seek the Lord through dialogue journaling as outlined above. Start with just a few questions. You might want to do identity one day, destiny the next, and assignment on yet another day. Don't try to do too much at once. Leave room for the Lord to truly speak, let things unfold, and give yourself time to listen.

Then, record your findings in the "Wrapping It Up" section at the end of today's work.

HOW DO I KNOW THIS IS GOD SPEAKING?

We hope you had a great experience with your first day of dialogue journaling. But, with an exercise like this, you may be asking, "Is this really God speaking—or am I just making it up?"

This is probably the most common question we get from those who are seeking the Lord but just beginning to hear Him speak.

First, we suggest that you go back to Day 1 of Step 5 and review the section titled, "Confirmation: Am I Sure?" This will help you develop a checklist for confirming what you hear. It will allow you to begin knowing and trusting the voice of God.

Second, there will be more about validation when you get to Step 7. We will provide additional guidance on how to make sure your purpose statements are truly God-given.

Finally, we suggest you take a test we call: "Could I possibly have written this without someone else's help?" To help you with this "test," consider the following excerpt from Erin James Sain's book *The Secret Place:*

> One day I said to my friend and spiritual mentor, Francis, "I just do not feel like God ever talks to me." He looked at me and then down at my opened Bible and laughed. It was barely readable. I had underlined, cross-referenced, highlighted, circled, and written thoughts on the empty spaces of almost every page! He motioned to the Bible and said, "If God is not speaking to you, then where did you get all that?"
>
> Those words were a huge wake up call. I had been presumptuous enough to think that I had just thought it all up! I then realized that the countless pages I had written, my understanding of the Word, and the fact that I even had hunger for the Word were all due to God's fellowship with me.
>
> From that day on, I looked at fellowship with God in a whole new light. I realized that I had many misconceptions about the ways of God. I began to understand that God speaks through a number of sources such as His Word, people, and circumstances, just to name a few. I had been waiting for the Lord to reveal Himself to me, unaware that He already had!

the ways of God

It may be that you are like this author. Has the Lord revealed Himself to you, yet you remain unaware of how He is speaking—or what He has already said?

THE MOST IMPORTANT THING

Please pray for wisdom and continue seeking the Lord. Keep using your spiritual disciplines and wait on the Lord.

It's also important to recognize that when you do work like you've done over the past six weeks; the greatest benefit may not be limited to learning your purpose. It may be the chance to draw near to the Lord, maybe closer than ever before.

And, as you continue toward the final step of the program, remember, the Lord doesn't normally lay out His plans with full details or step-by-step instructions. When He first called many of His servants and disciples, He simply said: "Follow Me." Knowing it was a call from the Lord was enough for them to drop what they were doing and begin to follow. You just need to stay with the disciplines, learn to recognize God's voice, and keep collecting all the beautiful pieces of your mosaic—one piece at a time, one day at a time.

As you've worked through **7 Steps to Purpose,** there is one more treasure you have had the chance to collect. You have had the chance to begin learning how to "remain in Him."

I am the vine; you are the branches. If a man remains in me and I in him, he will bear much fruit; apart from me you can do nothing…If you remain in me and my words remain in you, ask whatever you wish, and it will be given you. John 15:5, 8

The Lord is our vine—we are His branches. Without that kind of relationship, we cannot receive the nourishment we need or bear the kind of fruit He desires. These five disciplines will help you remain, or abide, in the Lord. It doesn't get any better than that!

WRAPPING IT UP

The only spiritual discipline you will be asked to work on today is dialogue journaling. Hopefully you have done the exercise as outlined above and are ready to summarize the highlights of what the Lord said that relates to your identity, destiny, or assignment. If not, please do so now.

Make a note here of the thoughts, feelings, words, pictures, or anything else you received as you did your first day of **dialogue journaling**:

A Little Extra Help:
If you feel like "writer's block" is holding you back in your dialogue journaling, listen for concepts and ideas, and watch for pictures or recurring themes. Just jot down notes as they appear. If nothing comes, write out a prayer asking for help and guidance. Sometimes just putting your pen in motion and putting something on paper starts the process. Other people discover that writing as though they're asking a friend for advice can also be helpful. Start with your own journaling, but remain open to what the Lord might want to say as you write.

But when he asks, he must believe and not doubt. James 1:6

Day 4 | *Can You "Be Still" and Listen?*

Today we'll start with meditation and then move on to another session of dialogue journaling. If you have time to employ the other disciplines, that's fine. But please give these two assignments your greatest attention.

Before diving into the exercises, let's take one more look at both meditation and dialogue journaling.

FOOD FOR THE SOUL

According to many teachers and theologians, meditation can be one of the deepest and most meaningful methods you will ever use in studying the Scriptures.

pass

peacefully

through

deep

trials

Christian evangelist and philanthropist George Muller, best known for his gift of faith, was also diligent about meditating on God's Word. In one of his journal entries he noted:

> "It often astonished me that I did not see the importance of meditation upon Scripture earlier in my Christian Life. As the outward man is not fit for work at any length of time unless he eats, so it is with the inner man. What is the food of the inner man? It is the Word of God. It is not the simple reading of the Word of God so that it only passes through our minds, just as water runs through a pipe. No, we must consider what we read, ponder over it, and apply it to our hearts.
>
> Through His Word, our Father speaks to us, encourages us, comforts us, instructs us, humbles us, and reproves us. Meditation strengthens our inner man. Meditation on God's Word has given me the help and strength to pass peacefully through deep trials. What a difference there is when the soul is refreshed in fellowship with God. Without spiritual preparation, the service, the trials, and the temptations of the day can be overwhelming."

We hope you have already begun to enjoy the power and insight of meditation. It truly is "food for the soul of your inner man."

A man does not live on bread alone but on every word that comes from the mouth of the LORD. Deuteronomy 8:3

FROM FEAR TO FAVORITE

Although you've had only one day to experience dialogue journaling, we hope you have begun to enjoy this discipline. We also hope you've been able to keep those "three amigos" in their proper place.

We say this because we know it can be rather difficult to really let go and give this discipline an honest try. To illustrate, let us share Jim's story.

Jim came to the **7 Step** program with a genuine desire to know his God-given purpose. He was comfortable with the Bible and regularly attended church, but he had never developed a daily routine of spending time with the Lord.

As the steps unfolded, Jim began to love the spiritual disciplines being taught. Unfortunately, when we got to dialogue journaling that's where he put on the brakes. He just couldn't get beyond the thought that he was the one doing the writing—NOT God.

After several coaching sessions, Tom asked him to give it one more try. He asked him to find a time when he could be alone for at least an hour and just get his pen on the paper and write. Tom said, "Don't worry about where it's coming from—just let go and have some fun."

Later that week, we got a call from Jim. He was so excited about what had begun to happen in his dialogue journaling that he couldn't wait until our next scheduled meeting to tell us.

Having checked into a hotel for an overnight business trip, he found time to give the process a try. He began with prayer and then simply began to write. As he finished, he realized he had nine pages of journaling and had been at it for two and a half hours! When he went back and read what was written, he was certain that the Lord's hand was driving the pen to write what was on those pages. He received information on his identity and destiny, but also a very specific assignment telling him to work on a particular personal issue before he would be released into the purpose the Lord had waiting.

That night, Jim knew the Lord had spoken directly to him. Needless to say, dialogue journaling is now a favorite discipline that he enjoys on a regular basis.

For Jim—and maybe for you—it might take a step of courage like this to go beyond your skepticism and fear, and trust that the Lord will join you in this process called dialogue journaling. Just put your pen to paper and give it a try.

You do the steps—God does the rest!

WRAPPING IT UP

Begin now with a little "food for your soul." Continue with **meditation** as instructed on Day 3 of Step 5.

Use the recommended verse below or a verse of your choosing.

Proverbs 19:21 Choose the version that resonates with you:	
King James Version	There are many devices in a man's heart; nevertheless the counsel of the LORD, that shall stand.
Amplified Bible	Many plans are in a man's mind, but it is the Lord's purpose for him that will stand.
New American Standard Bible	Many plans are in a man's heart, But the counsel of the LORD will stand.
New International Version	Many are the plans in a man's heart, but it is the LORD's purpose that prevails.

Jot down what you have learned through today's **meditation**. Don't forget, God may not speak in complete sentences. You're looking for thoughts, feelings, pictures, and places. Don't worry about whether it makes sense; it will all come together as you create the mosaic of your identity and destiny.

Now, let's take time to seek the Lord through **dialogue journaling** as outlined on Day 3 of Step 6. Just as we suggested yesterday, start with just a few questions. If you've worked on identity now go to destiny or assignment. Don't try to do too much at once. Leave room for the Lord to speak, let things unfold, and give yourself time to listen.

Do your journaling on a separate note pad or journal and record the highlights of what you learned below:

Finally, if you have received any **other messages, images, or information** from the Lord that go beyond today's exercises, please make a note of them here.

Day 5 | Can You "Be Still" and Listen?

Step 6 is coming to a close. **Well done!**

Next week, we'll start assembling your mosaic and crystallize your identity, destiny, and assignment statements. We will continue with another level of validation and then begin to talk about where you go from here.

But we're not quite ready for that yet. Let's begin today with a personal "time management" assessment:

1. Are you able to set aside the necessary time to do your **7 Steps** homework?
2. Do you spend time daily with the Lord using the disciplines being taught?
3. Do you find your relationship with the Lord getting deeper and more intimate as a result of the time you are spending with Him?

TOM'S APPROACH

We talked a lot about carving out the necessary time to do your assignments, but more importantly, to develop a relationship with the Lord where communication flows easily and freely. If that is not happening for you, odds are it is a question of your daily practices and time management.

In talking with many clients and program participants, we find it is not so much about managing your time throughout the day, but making sure you spend time with the Lord before your day begins. Your best shot at uninterrupted time with the Lord is before the appointments on your calendar get started and your to-do list takes over.

Tom suggests a routine that starts as soon as you rise. Don't turn on the television, don't grab the newspaper, and definitely don't check your email or operate any other electronic device. He says it's okay to make a cup of coffee, but keep yourself in a quiet state as you do it.

Find a quiet place. Begin with prayer and perhaps a daily Scripture or devotional. Then proceed with the spiritual disciplines you have chosen to work on that day. As Tom would say, "Plan your work—then work that plan!" You will be amazed by the results—and the quality of your day.

AN HONEST LOOK

Now, we want you to take an honest look at one more thing: how you approach God. Even once you have learned to "fear the Lord" and come into His presence with proper respect, you still need to be mindful of the tendency to turn your prayers into a time of nothing but petition, the opportunity to ask the Lord to meet your needs, solve your problems, or help you out of the latest bind.

God tells us in ***James 4:2: You have not, because you ask not.*** But if that is all you do when you are with Him, your relationship is seriously out of balance.

As Pastor Matthew says: "God is not our cosmic bell hop."

"stay tuned"

A wise counselor told us as she was teaching us about parenting: "Your relationship with your children will be healthy and mature when they see you for *who you can be*—rather than *what you can do* for them."

We think the Lord looks at things the same way. He wants to be there with you and for you, but He does not want to face an open palm waiting for a handout every time you approach Him.

Think about this as you talk with the Lord about your purpose. and think in terms of what He wants to tell you rather than asking Him to bless and confirm the plans you've already made. Your questions need to be open-ended, allowing the Lord the opportunity to reveal truths about Himself, His activity, and the plan He has for you.

PURPOSE NOT PIZZA

A final word of caution from our often-quoted resource, Henry Blackaby:

> "Some skeptics have asked questions such as: "Do you need to pray and ask God what type of toothpaste you should purchase at the store?" Such questions reveal a fundamental lack of understanding about why God speaks. Unless your choice of toothpaste affects Christ's lordship in your life, it is undoubtedly of no consequence to God. Our choice of spouse, career or place to live, on the other hand, dramatically impacts how we can serve Christ in the future. Whether we decide to order a cheeseburger or pizza for dinner will not alter eternity. Placing ourselves in crippling debt to start our own business may be important to God if it prevents us from fulfilling His future assignment for us. Ultimately our lives will be enriched by focusing on Him rather than focusing on ourselves. The most important truths God communicates are the truths about what He is like and what His purposes are."

STAY TUNED

As you solidify your daily routine with the Lord and get comfortable with the ways He speaks to you, we also want to encourage you to stay tuned as you go through the day. Get in the habit of writing down any thoughts that seem to pop into your mind, even if you're not consciously asking the Lord for guidance at the time. God will choose His own time and His own way of talking to you!

countless ways to enjoy the Lord

As you learned yesterday from John 15, when your relationship with the Lord deepens, you will actually begin to "remain" with Him throughout the day, and He will "remain" with you. If you learn to go about your day in a constant state of listening prayer, you will be amazed by what you begin to hear. Eventually, your time with the Lord will not be limited to a particular time of day or spiritual discipline. It will be a growing, vibrant relationship with the Lord that becomes a way of life.

We hope you are finding success with the five disciplines, and we hope you see that they are not the end-all for hearing God's voice. They are simply our way of giving you a firm foundation from which to grow. There are countless ways to enjoy the Lord and the time you spend with Him.

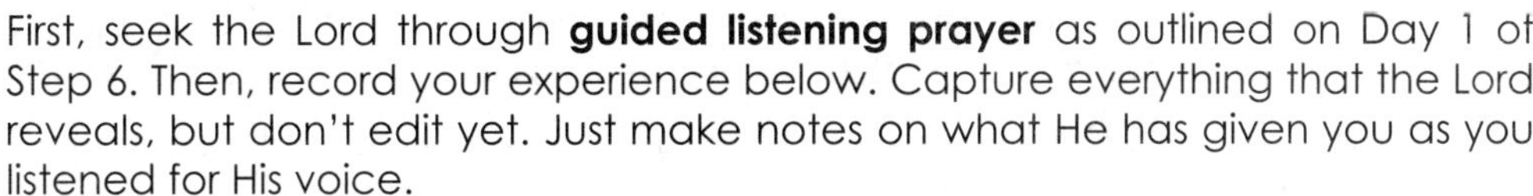

WRAPPING IT UP

Let's keep growing by spending time today in guided listening prayer and dialogue journaling.

First, seek the Lord through **guided listening prayer** as outlined on Day 1 of Step 6. Then, record your experience below. Capture everything that the Lord reveals, but don't edit yet. Just make notes on what He has given you as you listened for His voice.

Now, let's take time to seek the Lord through **dialogue journaling** as outlined on Day 3 of Step 6. Just as we suggested earlier, start with just a few questions. If you've worked on identity and destiny, now go to assignment. Don't try to do too much at once. Leave room for the Lord, let things unfold, and give yourself time to listen.

Do your journaling on a separate note pad or journal and record the highlights of what you learned below:

Finally, if you have received any **other messages, images or information** from the Lord that goes beyond today's meditation and guided listening prayer — please make a note of it here.

Review | *Can You "Be Still" and Listen?*

KEY POINTS TO REMEMBER!

- Guided listening prayer and dialogue journaling are the disciplines that most often bring the greatest level of results and insight.
- Be quiet and God's whisper will come to you without fail, and you will know it when He speaks.
- Silence may be a means of God deepening His relationship with you—it might even be one of the ways He chooses to communicate.
- We do not all hear the Lord in the same way. Stay open and attentive to the limitless ways He may choose to speak.
- Really letting go—and giving each of the spiritual disciplines an honest effort—can sometimes be difficult. Step out with courage and trust the Lord to honor your perseverance.
- Learning and continuing to practice the five spiritual disciplines can stretch your understanding of the Lord and His wonderful plan for your life. Carve out the time and enjoy the journey!
- God wants you to know Him and learn to hear His voice. When that happens, it will change your life forever!

My Big "Aha"
What was the most dramatic or important thing you learned this week?

Capture It!
Go back through your notes and record the most important words, phrases, pictures, feelings, concepts, and key thoughts that have come from your week's work.

God's Word
Identify the Scripture that impacted you most deeply this week and journal your thoughts in the following format:

Write out the Scripture:

Identify its **message** to you:

How can you **apply** that to your life?

Write a **prayer** back to the Lord about this Scripture. Thank Him, ask for help, or just talk it through, whatever feels right.

Personal Notes, Thoughts, and Journaling

STEP 7 | WEEK EIGHT

Who Am I? and Why Am I Here?

ASSEMBLE THE MOSAIC

CRYSTALLIZE YOUR PURPOSE STATEMENTS

VALIDATION AND NEXT STEPS

THE CHALLENGE

Day 1 & 2 | *Who Am I? and Why Am I Here?*

ARE WE THERE YET?

Step 7, Week 8. We're finally nearing the end of our journey, and what an amazing journey it has been! Thank you for all your hard work, and thanks for hanging in there.

As with every journey, we can all get a little tired, a little anxious, a little like children on a long road trip asking, "Are we there yet?!?" Our answer is much like that of a parent: "It's just a little while longer, but it will all be worth it."

what an amazing journey

You will begin Step 7 by gathering and organizing all the pieces of your purpose mosaic, then you will finally assemble your masterpiece. You will crystallize your identity and destiny statements, and once written, you will know with certainty who God created you to be and what He has gifted you to do. You will be able to answer the two universal questions that started your journey: "Who am I?" and "Why am I here?"

You'll also spend time clarifying any assignments God may have given. The focus will be not only on your assignments, but knowing when, and if, God has actually given you one. Most people receive assignments that take the form of personal action steps or short-term tasks or projects. If you are expecting something "big and glamorous," you may easily overlook what God is assigning next. Regardless of where you are on the continuing road of personal and spiritual development—assignments are often God's way of preparing you for what lies ahead and deepening your relationship with Him.

ENJOY THE JOURNEY

Some years back we found ourselves getting more and more frustrated with the hassles of travel—especially airline travel after 9.11.01. It was beginning to take all the fun out of our trips—even if they were for vacation rather than business. After a few years of letting this attitude get the best of us, we decided it was time for a change. It was time to begin enjoying the journey. From that point on, we would plan more stops along the way, pack good food to take on board, and save frequent flyer points and upgrade to first class whenever possible. We took things like movies and books on tape that we knew we would enjoy doing together. But most of all, we simply made a conscious choice to begin having fun the moment we left the house—no longer waiting until we reached our destination.

We hope that's how you've been able to look at the **7 Steps to Purpose** as you've traveled the past seven weeks of your journey. You've covered a lot of ground and learned a great deal. You've taken a long and careful look at the gifts God has given you, the many blessings you have received, and the character traits that make you unique, yet perfectly created by God.

Many of you have gone back to times in your lives that were very difficult, but hopefully you've reconsidered those events, realized you've come through them a stronger, better person, and recognized them as crucial to the purpose God has planned.

A LOOK BACK

Before we charge off to our final destination, let's take a look back to see just how far we've come and recall all the good things that happened along the way:

In Week 1, we welcomed you on board and began with the questionnaire: "Are You Living on Purpose?" Once you had a snapshot of where you were starting, we moved on to a two-part review to detail the benefits of knowing your God-given purpose.

Step 1 took a look at how you are wired. We had some fun with your Personality Style Analysis, revealing your strongest DISC behavioral language and the "character" that best describes you. Then you learned how to use your style effectively and adapt to the styles of others for improved relationships and communication. We then went on to assess your Resilience Quotient and determine your ability to overcome obstacles, bounce back from adversity, and steer through difficulties. We took a look at how to improve critical skills for dealing with a real world with real struggles.

Step 2 led us down the path of understanding what makes you tick. We took a hard look at your core values and beliefs, narrowing them down to those you chose based on sound wisdom rather than those you felt you should adopt because others pushed them on you. Then we moved into the process of identifying your dominant spiritual gift, and the character traits and blessings that come along with it. We also tucked away some insight into the needs and desires that go along with your area of gifting, as well as, a few things to look out for if your gift is taken to extremes.

Step 3 took us on a trip down memory lane and the discovery of your passions. We looked back at past experiences, people, and events that have influenced you, things you hope to accomplish, and wrongs you want to make right—all to find the things you are deeply passionate about. We then took a look at the needs underlying your passion and discovered how they also point to your purpose.

Step 4 took us across "the bridge," leading from the intellectual to the spiritual phase of the journey still ahead. The bridge took us over some pretty rough waters, but smoothed a path to purpose that could not be cleared any other way. We had to look fears, blocks, and limiting beliefs square in the face and find the weapons we needed to conquer them. The weapon of choice: the truth of God's Word as found in Scripture.

Step 5 began with the most important action step of all: your personal prayer of commitment. This is where we helped you make the personal choice to truly surrender to the plans God has for your life and redefine "willpower." Then we began working with three spiritual disciplines designed to help you seek the Lord and hear Him speak, including purposeful prayer, meditation and dreams. On Day 1 of Step 5, we also picked up 14 important pointers to help you **prepare** to hear, **listen** for, and **confirm** the voice of God.

Step 6 took us deeper into the spiritual disciplines with guided listening prayer and dialogue journaling. This is the part of your journey that may have required an extra dose of courage and faith as you let go and really let things flow. But odds are these disciplines brought the greatest results and insight! Ultimately, as we wrapped up this leg of the journey, we learned that seeking the Lord and hearing what He has to say is all about relationship. He wants to tell us about our purpose, but above anything else He wants us to "remain" in Him and learn to treasure that relationship most of all!

surrender

to the

plans

WHAT A GIFT!

Wow! We really have covered a lot of ground! We haven't yet reached our destination, and look how much you've already learned. Look at all you discovered about yourself, the Lord, and how He looks at purpose. Just think about all the changes you have begun to make, and the work God has been able to do in your life. And you can be certain these new understandings and beliefs will continue to bring positive change in every area of your life.

We are now going to bring it all together, but even if we were to conclude right now you have a wealth of knowledge and understanding that few people will ever have a chance to gather. And it's all captured right here in the book you hold in your hands. We encourage you to keep this book and refer to it often. It is full of tools we hope you will continue to use, personal insight and understanding, and especially, notes and journaling that recap some very precious time spent with the Lord. Your completed **7 Step** workbook: what a gift!

SORTING AND ORGANIZING

Now we'll begin to organize the vast amount of information you have compiled into categories that will help clarify your identity, destiny, and assignments.

As has been the rule through the entire **7 Steps to Purpose**, there are no right or wrong answers. Breaking down the bits and pieces of your life into defined categories is more art than science, so don't get too hung up about doing it "exactly right." We're back to the first step in the process that was outlined early on: sorting and separating the colors, shapes, and textures of the pieces to be used in your mosaic. Once organized, we will then be able to crystallize and actually write out statements for the three elements of your purpose: identity, destiny, and assignment.

Every piece of information you have gathered is meaningful, but the most valuable is the insight and communication you've received from God over the last two weeks. Remember, the fundamental difference that sets the **7 Steps to Purpose** apart is seeking God directly. You will find that the information gleaned from your prayerful requests for guidance provide the deepest understanding and strongest indicators of how God wants to use you. As we've said before: "If you want to know what you were created to do, ask your Creator."

By sorting and organizing the pieces of your mosaic, you will begin to see how the information gained from the intellectual exercises is supported by the spiritual aspects of your discovery. It is only with spiritual discernment and direct communication from the Lord that you can fully comprehend how to use your gifts, blessings, and life experience in the way He has planned for your future.

SORTING EXERCISE

Instructions:
As we did with the Passion Pursuit, we will be doing this exercise over two days. We don't want you to hurry. Take your time, enjoy the journey, and ask the Lord to help you gather everything He wants you to consider. Begin by praying and asking the Lord to be with you and help with the sorting.

Start the process by going back through your workbook, looking especially at the "Wrapping It Up" sections at the end of each day and your notes in the "Review" sections at the end of each week. Be sure to review any other notes or journals you've kept along the way as well.

You'll need to go back through the workbook at least three times, looking for the three elements of purpose. Most people review it a fourth time to look for the miscellaneous directions God has given.

Use a different colored marker to highlight the different elements. For instance, mark all your identity information in yellow, destiny in orange, and your assignment information in green. This will make it much easier to transfer your information to the proper sorting page when it comes time to summarize.

The end goal of the sorting exercise is to take what you find in your workbook (and other notes and journals) and condense it down onto the following sorting pages, by category, as outlined below:

God made you perfectly

IDENTITY: Who am I? These are "being" statements, what you *are* and not what you *do*. It is your essence, who you are at your very core.

Examples:
- Strong
- Focused
- Joyful
- Peacemaker

DESTINY: Why am I here? This is what you do when you are just being you. It is not your job or position but a fundamental part of who you are—no matter what task, role, or activity in which you are involved. It is usually an action, a verb. It is the work of the Holy Spirit in the world through you!

Examples:
- Help
- Teach
- Guide
- Share

ASSIGNMENTS: These are projects or tasks. It could be a lifetime assignment or only for a certain season of your life. You may have one, you may have many, you may not always have one—it is up to God and His perfect timing.

Additional Sorting Categories: Information that goes beyond identity, destiny, and assignment might include the following:

INSTRUCTIONS: This heading is for any direct instruction you might have received, particularly relating to health, relationships, professional career, etc.

Examples:
- Be courageous
- Lose weight
- Develop skill
- Seek help

WHO: If you received insight on whom you are to serve, put it under this heading. This could be things like people in transition, lost people, hurting souls. The list is endless.

MESSAGE: Place any information about the specific message you are to take to the group you have been selected to serve. The message God gave us as we created this program was: "God made you perfectly just the way you are... now run with it!"

Our prayer is that the **7 Steps to Purpose** is helping you do exactly that.

IMAGES: Pictures or visions.

INFORMATION/MISCELLANEOUS: Use this to catch data that doesn't fit into other categories.

Finally, with your highlighted notes in hand, start filling out the Sorting Pages that begin on the next page. Some thoughts will obviously go in one place while others are less clear. You don't need to include every note from Steps 1 to 6 in the booklet and you may include some statements under more than one heading.

As you go through this assignment, remember that your sorting pages are designed to capture the words, phrases, pictures, and/or feelings you received as you went through the **7 Steps to Purpose**. Stay away from editing— this will come later.

And keep praying! Continue to use the five spiritual disciplines you've learned over the past two weeks and add anything new to these lists. Focus on the first three entries: identify, destiny, and assignment, whenever possible—and don't be concerned about how you received the information. You'll validate it in upcoming sessions.

Now, prayerfully begin your sorting exercise. And, remember, this exercise is meant to be done over two days. Take today and tomorrow to enjoy this part of the journey. You're going to be amazed by all you find as you go back and gather this information.

SORTING PAGE

IDENTITY (I Am...) Being, not doing:

SORTING PAGE

DESTINY (My destiny is to…) This is the work of the Holy Spirit in the world through you:

SORTING PAGE

ASSIGNMENT: What is my current assignment or task?

SORTING PAGE

INSTRUCTIONS that do not rise to the level of an assignment:

WHO is my purpose to be applied toward?

MESSAGE: If you were told to share a message to the world or perform public speaking, seminars, etc., what is your message?

IMAGES: This information might come from dreams or meditation.

INFORMATION/MISCELLANEOUS: Items that don't seem to fit into the other categories but appear to be important.

Day 3 | Who Am I? and Why Am I Here?

Finally, the moment you have been working toward is here! Now that you have organized your information onto the sorting pages, it is time to create purpose statements.

As you review your sorting pages, we encourage you to carefully consider every piece of information. For those who have pages overflowing with information, the work ahead will be one of narrowing it down to the core truth that God wants to reveal about each element of your purpose.

keep
moving
forward

But, for those who feel they don't have as much on their pages as they would like—or feel the Lord has not yet really spoken clearly—we want to encourage you to confidently keep moving forward with the information you've received thus far. In Steps 1 to 3 alone, you received enough knowledge and insight to begin creating your purpose statements. Diligently work through today's assignment, and continue seeking the Lord regarding your purpose. Ask Him to guide you as you create your statements, and trust that He will join you in the process.

We've seen God use the process of creating purpose statements as yet another powerful way of revealing purpose!

CREATING PURPOSE STATEMENTS

Instructions:
Review all the information in your sorting pages, prayerfully asking the Lord to guide you as you create your statements. Remember: we are seeking God's purpose for your life so don't cut Him out of the journey now. This is your chance to hear directly from God as He actually speaks a blessing over your life through your purpose statements.

Be encouraged! God wants you to come to Him, He wants you to know why He created you, and He definitely wants you to live the purpose He planned and created you to live!

Ask and you will be given, seek and you will find, knock and the door will be opened. Matthew 7:7

If anyone lacks wisdom, he should ask God, who gives generously to all without finding fault...But when he asks, he must believe and not doubt. James 1:4-5

Write down a series of statements from the information on the sorting page that applies to the element of purpose you are working to create. Be open and creative. Just let it flow. Begin by generating three, four, or five statements—as many as you can for each element of your purpose.

IDENTITY: We will start by creating your identity statements completing the sentence: "I am...." Remember, identity is the very core of who you are. Write down a series of identity statements from the information on your sorting page. If you received words like "love" or "peace," use those along with bridge words like "a source of," "a tool of," or "a gift of," etc.

Examples of Identity

- I am a source of peace.
- I am a beacon of love.
- I am an agent of change.
- I am a leader of truth.
- I am a tool of enlightenment.
- I am a peacemaker.
- I am a resilient survivor.

Now that you have a list of identity statements, use several of the spiritual disciplines you've learned in the **7 Steps** program to ask God for His insight on your statements. Don't worry if no single statement seems to be just right, we'll continue to work on honing them down to your pure God-given essence! The objective is to begin seeking confirmation from the Lord on the statements you've received thus far.

your pure God-given essence

DESTINY: Using the same process, create a series of destiny statements. In simple, clear terms complete the sentence: "My destiny (or purpose) is to...." These statements are to be a reflection of the work that the Holy Spirit wants to do in the world through you.

Try to avoid extraneous details such as the groups with whom you will work, specific details on how you will do it, etc. We will deal with those issues later. Your destiny statement should be a distillation of what you uniquely bring to the world.

Go back through your color-coded notes looking for destiny statements that reflect why God has created you. Stay away from job titles and professional roles. Your destiny is deeper than that, and can be exercised in many different roles.

Examples: My destiny (or purpose) is to...

- Be a positive influence on the lives of women and children.
- Heal people's aches.
- Show people their true selves.
- Love and honor others while guiding them to a better understanding of themselves.
- Help others use life's hurts and struggles as a source of growth, strength, and empowerment.
- Empower others through personal example to become mighty in spirit.
- Help others find a place of peace that is soul deep.

listen,

trust and

obey

Keep praying! Use your spiritual disciplines to seek the Lord for confirmation and continued wisdom, knowledge, and insight. List your destiny statements below.

ASSIGNMENT: Typically, this is easier than the first two statements, probably because it seems to be more natural to grasp the idea of "doing something."

But don't forget that although your assignment is a very important part of your purpose, the first two statements are much more critical! They are the parts of your purpose that truly answer the questions: Who am I?" and "Why am I here?" You can be living your identity and destiny without a specific task or assignment.

Return to your sorting booklet for inspiration and write several statements to complete the phrase "My assignment is to...." Focus on words, thoughts, and themes given to you by the Lord over the last two weeks but also consider your core values, dominant spiritual gift, and strongest passions as well.

Example: One of the most important assignments given in Scripture is when God spoke to Moses.

So now, go, I am sending you to Pharaoh to bring my people, the Israelites, out of Egypt. Exodus 3:10

God did not give specifics on how long this would take, how it was to be accomplished, or the details of what was involved. He simply gave Moses the next step in the process. When Moses showed he was ready to obey this one assignment—only then was more given.

continue to pray and seek

Don't start worrying about how big or small your assignment may be, or the details of how to make it happen. For now, just capture any assignments you feel God has given.

Also remember that your assignment may not be what you expected and your current assignment may not be the "end game." Just like Moses, most of us receive assignments that are only part of the larger plan that God has for our lives. He may very well be giving you assignments that are part of your preparation for the full-blown purpose He has for you. And, as you begin to walk in the spirit and live according to God's plan for your life, you will find He rarely gives the big picture all at once.

In God's economy, it is very often one day at a time. You may find this difficult at first, but once you get used to it, living according to God's timing and plans can be a very exciting way to live! It is important to simply keep listening, trust His plan, and obey His next instruction.

Examples of Assignment

- Create 1,000 other partners to spread the message of self-acceptance.
- Make abiding disciples of Jesus Christ who will also be qualified to make abiding disciples of Jesus Christ.
- Seek help to overcome the long-held areas of bitterness and unforgiveness that are holding me back.
- Make every effort to restore my marriage—putting first things first.
- Really live and use my identity and destiny statements, learning to recognize every opportunity to do so.

If you received an assignment or task from the Lord, write it here.

CAMP OUT IF YOU NEED TO

We hope today's exercise of creating your purpose statements has produced good results. You should have a strong list of possible purpose statements for both identity and destiny. You should also have any assignments God has revealed over the past seven weeks.

If you feel there is still some work to be done on your lists, please feel free to "camp out" on this step a day or two longer. At this point, taking time to capture all your possible purpose statements is important enough to slow things down, if necessary.

Continue to pray and seek the Lord. Review your sorting pages. Go back and take one more look through your notes in the "Wrapping It Up" and "Review" sections of your workbook.

If you feel like today's lists bring excitement and energy when you read over them, press on! But if you need a little extra time, that's okay too. We don't want you to miss anything God might want you to consider.

The next step will be narrowing down the information you have gathered even further. Tomorrow we will capture the one statement that really resonates with spiritual power. Get ready. It's going to be an amazing day!

Day 4 | Who Am I? and Why Am I Here?

real power and authenticity

Now that you've created a series of identity and destiny statements, you'll go back to the Lord in prayer to crystallize those thoughts and connect on a spiritual level with identity, destiny, and assignment statements that have real power and authenticity.

Don't worry if you don't have lists that are as complete as you would like, just go with what God has already given. Trust that He will provide anything else that is needed as you faithfully continue to work through the process.

You do the steps—God does the rest!

IDENTIFYING YOUR PURPOSE STATEMENTS

Instructions:

1. Go back to the individual sheets you completed yesterday with the lists of potential identity, destiny, and assignment statements. Go through each one separately as described below.

2. Relax in a comfortable chair, preferably a spot where you can lean your head back. Put the "three amigos" in the "Crystal Box" so that you can concentrate on God instead of hearing their skeptical, critical, and judgmental voices.

3. Close your eyes and prayerfully ask God for His guidance.

4. Take each of your **Identity** statements—one at a time. Read the statement out loud, close your eyes, meditate on what you have just read, then rate your physical and emotional response to that statement. Rate your reaction on a scale of 1 to 5 (1 being no response to 5 being a very strong, high-energy response). Make a note of the response level beside that statement.

5. Go through the entire list. Listen and be careful to recognize how He is speaking to you in your thoughts and the physical and emotional response you have to these statements.

6. After you have rated all of your identity statements, you will probably have three or four with high ratings. Repeat the process for each of the high-rated statements and see if one rises above all the others in terms of the strongest response. If so, count this as your "winner." We will be doing further validation with the Lord and others who know and care about you, but if you have narrowed it down to one statement, you have preliminarily identified this element of your purpose.

7. If you end up with multiple statements with equally high ratings, take a look at all of them with an eye on contrast and comparison. Do you see common themes, words, concepts, or emphasis? Is there a way to combine or rearrange them into a single statement that will really hit the mark? Remember to keep praying—you're asking God for your purpose and you must keep your mind open to His voice if you expect Him to participate in the process.

Repeat this process for your **Destiny** and **Assignment** statements until you have isolated the winners in each category.

DIVE DEEPER

Like some other areas in the **7 Steps to Purpose**, it may be best to work through the process of identifying your final purpose statements with a trained coach. Dive deeper if you would like a little extra help. Visit the Resources area of www.IdentityandDestiny.com to learn more about the coaches who have completed our certified training programs to provide "laser coaching" sessions.

YOUR PURPOSE STATEMENTS

Once you have successfully completed today's work and selected the winning statement for each element of purpose, write them out by completing the sentences below:

IDENTITY
I am...

DESTINY
My destiny is to...

ASSIGNMENT
My assignment is to...

Congratulations! Next, we will validate your statements.

THE VALIDATION PROCESS

Start by standing up, taking a deep breath, and reading your identity statement out loud with conviction and gusto. Listen to yourself and connect with the emotional response you are having as you read your statements.

How do you feel? Is there real energy and power behind this statement? Can you feel God's strength and affirmation backing it up? Many people will actually have a very strong physical response. The hair on the back of your neck may rise, your heart may be beating faster, or you may feel the tears start to well-up.

Make a note of your thoughts and feelings:

Now, repeat this same validation exercise for your destiny statement. Once you have done so, make a note of your thoughts and feelings:

Do not accept a statement that has no energy!

If you are not feeling energy, it is likely that you are still trying to create your statements from your head and not your heart. You may also be trying to do this intellectually rather than spiritually. Go back to the Lord in prayer and ask Him to fully express His wishes for your life. Ask Him to help you find and know your purpose. Ask Him to make sure you are receiving His wisdom rather than trying to create this on your own.

Remember, less is always better.

Don't try to put too much information into your identity and destiny statements. Review the examples provided in this week's assignments and notice that they are only one short sentence in length. As we noted when we started this process, the goal is discovering God's purpose for your life—not creating a "ready for publication" branding or marketing statement.

We recognize how easy it is to put too much information into your purpose statement, to make it more flowery, to create something you're pleased to share with your family and friends. That's not what's important here!

Go back one more time and verify your winning statements by reviewing them in comparison to all the statements you originally created. Reconsider every statement to make sure you did not eliminate or include statements based on conscious evaluation alone. Remember we are seeking God, not 'self,' for the answers!

don't lose what you've captured

Step back and simply soak in the statements you have created. Pray and allow God to bless you with answers to the questions of "Who am I?" and "Why am I here?" This isn't about the details of how, when, or where. For now we want purpose statements that define the core of who you are and how the Holy Spirit wants to work in the world through you.

If you're perfectly comfortable that God has shared your identity and destiny statements, you now have our permission to do a little "wordsmithing." But, don't lose what you have captured. Be careful not to water down or embellish these statements to the point you lose your original emotional and physical response. If you lose it, you will have lost an important indicator that you're truly linked to the purpose God has for your life.

FINAL STEPS OF VALIDATION

You're almost there! You just have two more steps to verify and validate your statements.

Go to God using **guided listening prayer** and **dialogue journaling** to ask the Lord if your identity and destiny statements are His. Ask Him if they are an accurate reflection of the purpose He has for your life. Also ask Him if you have received your assignments correctly. Write the results of your conversations with God here:

Finally, we want you to validate your statements with three or four people who know you very well.

fully

integrate

purpose

If you have been working through the **7 Steps to Purpose** in a small study group, this validation may have been happening all along. If not, think of three or four friends who know you well enough that they would be able to hear your statements and assess them against the "you" they know and love.

Remember, you are not asking these confidants to edit or rewrite, just validate.

Share the statements you have received from God, and ask your friends if they think they are a good fit. People who love you and see your day-to-day activities probably have a very good insight into how God has blessed you and how you share His love in the world. They are not the authority on accuracy, but they can be a valuable part of confirmation.

YOU'VE ARRIVED!

There's only one day remaining on our journey, and you should now have your purpose statements crystallized and confirmed. Our final challenge:

Make your God-given purpose statements a way of life!

Tomorrow, as we conclude, we'll introduce steps that can be taken to begin fully integrating purpose into your life. Now that you know your purpose, we want to lay out a course of action that will help you really live it.

Before closing today's work, we want to offer a few words of encouragement to anyone who's still struggling to finalize their purpose statements:

DIVE DEEPER

In a recent interview, author John Eldridge was talking about how to hear the voice of God in his book *Walking With God*. Eldridge offered step-by-step instructions for learning to hear God's voice, and said, "Yes, God speaks! And you can all learn to hear his voice."

Eldridge believes that the key is starting with simple questions, getting comfortable with the idea of hearing from God, and realizing it is a voice that will come from your heart. He says internal surrender is critical, and we must be willing to hear God say "no" if we are ever going to hear him say "yes." Eldridge says you must walk before you run and you must understand that "God is after intimacy—while we're usually after answers." You can find more about Eldridge's book on our site at the Resources area of www.IdentityandDestiny.com.

Day 5 | *Who Am I? and Why Am I Here?*

THANK YOU LORD!

Our purposeful God has given us the privilege of creating the **7 Steps to Purpose**, writing this workbook, and being your personal guides on what has hopefully been a life-altering, attention-focusing journey of discovery.

Thank you for the honor of spending this time together, and thanks be to God for the opportunity to experience and express our purpose in such a meaningful and fulfilling way!

Tom's Identity: I am a source of strength and focus.

Tom's Destiny: To love and honor others by guiding them to a better understanding of themselves.

Pam's Identity: I am a peacemaker.

Pam's Destiny: To help others find a place of peace that is soul deep.

Our Assignments:

- To create 1,000 other partners to spread the message of self-acceptance.
- To spread the message: "You're okay just the way God made you, now run with what you have."

Here is a bit more of our story:

As God so often does, He gave us our purpose statements and assignments before He began to reveal the **7 Step** program. When He first helped us bring this step-by-step process together, it was designed for one-on-one coaching and small groups. It wasn't until several years later that He began to talk to us about writing a book. As we are finishing the book, He is just now beginning to bring people, resources, and insight about how He wants us to accomplish the assignment of creating 1,000 partners. But one thing is for sure: we trust that He has things already underway, and getting this workbook published and distributed is simply our next step in the process.

Throughout the process, God has made several things clear:

- If we are going to teach the phrase, "You do the Steps—God does the Rest," He wants us to live it!
- When God gave us this underlying principle for the **7 Step** program we knew right away that it was more than just a catchy phrase. We quickly learned that He would provide ample opportunities for us to actually live and experience this truth.

It has also become evident that God was going to teach us how to live step-by-step with Him. In all honesty, it was a bit hard to get used to not clearly knowing our next step well in advance. Over time, we discovered that it's not just an exciting way to live but that it has greatly reduced our worry and stress! We have actually gotten to the point where a lack of clarity or certainty becomes an opportunity to seek, listen, wait, and trust. We have begun to gratefully accept that God is applying this principle to our lives knowing we would otherwise tend to take matters into our own hands and likely miss His all-important guidance, wisdom, and direction.

it is always about relationship

The other thing God has made clear is that no matter how busy we are in our activity for Him, we must always remember He has led us to the experience in order to bring us closer to Him! It is always about relationship. It is always about learning to abide and remain in Him.

As we continue to live our identity and destiny and accomplish the assignments He has given to us, God has shown himself to be faithful and trustworthy. He has shown us, beyond a shadow of a doubt, if we do the steps...He will do the rest!

As you begin thinking about how to live your God-given purpose and complete your assignments, this basic underlying principle of the **7 Steps to Purpose** is worth committing to memory and following daily:

You do the Steps—God does the Rest!

VERIFICATION AND VALIDATION

Instructions:
Today we want to provide one more opportunity to verify and validate your purpose statements. Go through the following checklist as outlined below:

1. Go back and make sure your purpose statements are in alignment with the themes you discovered in your passion pursuit, core values, and dominant spiritual gift inventory.

2. Verify that people who know you well agree that your skills and passions are expressed in your purpose statements and that your close friends and family members think your purpose statements are a "good fit."

3. As you look back over your life, can you see that God has used your past experience and life events as a training ground for your purpose?

4. Have the spiritual disciplines you've used allowed you to get positive confirmation from the Lord about your identity, destiny, and assignment statements?

5. Do your purpose statements "feel right"? Do they generate peace in your spirit?

6. Stand up and read your statements out loud. Do you continue to have a strong emotional reaction to your purpose statements?

7. As you live your purpose statements, do you feel energy and passion? Do they give you a clear plumb line against which to make choices and decisions?

The last two points on this validation checklist are verifications you should continue to use on a regular basis. Reading—and ultimately memorizing—your purpose statements is a MUST! Say them out loud every day—with energy and gusto. You have to really own these statements. They have to be woven into the fabric of how you look at yourself and the things you choose to do in life. Your God-given purpose is who you are and why you are here. Now you need to live it!

ONE MORE QUESTION

Before we begin wrapping things up on this final day together, let's address a couple of questions you may still be asking:

"What if my purpose statements aren't completely accurate?"

"What if I missed what God wants me to know?"

do not

give up

Joyce Meyer says this was a big concern of hers when she was first hearing God's call to full-time ministry. She would spend hours asking God, "What if I miss you?" She loved the Lord and really wanted to hear him correctly. She really wanted to get it "right." So, as she continued to ask, God finally said to her, "Don't worry, Joyce, if you miss me, I will find you. Even if you get off on the wrong track, I will use it all for good. I will get you back on track."

As long as you have truly been seeking the Lord and as long as you have done all the recommended confirmation and validation exercises, we suggest that you just go with what you've got. If you experience passion, energy, and excitement when you recite and begin to live your defined purpose, then we are certain that God has both the desire and the power to steer you back onto the right path if you've missed it. Keep asking and seeking—the door will be opened.

As you go forward, use your gifts, apply all your life experience, and trust that God is moving you toward the purpose He has for your life. Continue to use the spiritual disciplines and do not give up the habit of meeting with Him daily in a solitary place.

You know that above all things, the Lord wants to have an intimate love relationship with you. As that relationship grows and deepens, your ability to hear His voice and trust what you hear will grow and deepen. And, although this phase of your journey is coming to a close, your journey to a life lived on purpose has only begun. And most importantly, your journey to an abiding intimacy with the Lord is meant to last forever.

LIVING ON PURPOSE

If you are still wondering what a life lived on purpose really looks like, let us share a few more stories from others who have completed the **7 Steps to Purpose:**

Skip says:
"It has made all the difference in what I am currently doing. I have become addicted to the journaling and often do 8 to 10 pages. *Identity and Destiny* has been a turning point in my faith journey. I find myself to be less stressed. It is beyond words what it has done for me. Absolutely wonderful!!!"

Rod says:
"During the last week or so I have been meditating on my purpose statements, and I see how they have been part of my past and now energize me for the future. I can say confidently I have validation from the Lord on my purpose. "As I have begun to live my life on purpose, I have much more focus, energy, and peace in my life. I'm enjoying the freedom to be who God created me to be. *Identity and Destiny* has taken my walk with God to a whole new level. I relish the closeness and the privilege I have to pray continuously and truly believe I have the skills to hear from God."

Carolyn says:
"I owned a business for seven years but it no longer felt 'right.' I wasn't sure what was out of alignment or what to do next. Thanks to your program I was able to identify my core values and clarify why I was losing interest in my work. Even more importantly, I was able to articulate my identity and my calling. I now have a compass for whatever business I choose to start next. "*Identity and Destiny* has helped me become more in tune with myself as well as my relationship with God. You gave me new tools and methods for strengthening that relationship, which is going far beyond the time spent working the program."

Tim says:
"The *Identity and Destiny* program was both confirming and enlightening. It helped me create a clear picture of myself, how I am wired, and how I process information and events. But, the one thing I *never* really expected from the program was how it helped me bring my spiritual maturity to a whole new level. The dialogue journaling is a great tool, and prior to this I hated to journal. It is a tool I now use on a regular basis to process problems, make decisions, and go to God about anything and everything."

Buddy says:
"Years of venturing, parenting, politicking, and growing gave me a pretty good sense of who I am, but I wanted a simple 'word filter' in my soul, through which I could consider all the choices before me. I wanted a better way to determine—with God's help—what fits ME. Though initially skeptical, I followed the program. It was a simple, yet amazingly profound walk to the 'defining descriptor' I needed. "It was nothing spooky or mystical—yet just shy of miraculous! My investment in time and energy was well worth it many times over. It is invaluable to find, in a few words, who you REALLY are."

WHAT'S YOUR STORY?

With these stories—and every new story we receive—we thank God for the amazing work He is doing through the **7 Steps to Purpose**. Lives are being changed, relationships with the Lord are being deepened, and the purposes of God are actually being discovered and lived out. We are humbled, amazed, and so very grateful to be used by God in this work!

We know you have a story also. We hope you will go to our blog and share it with us. If you will accept this assignment, or better yet, our request for a favor, please go today and post your comments on our blog at www.IdentityandDestiny.com/blog. Tell us about your **7 Steps** experience and share your God-given identity and destiny statements with us. Let us know how your life has been impacted and what has changed. And even though we're using computer technology, this can be our way of continuing to meet and encourage one another.

Let us not give up meeting together, as some are in the habit of doing, but let us encourage one another. Hebrews 10:25

lives changed... relationships deepened... purpose discovered

We hope you will visit our blog often and keep us updated on how God uses you and your purpose.

ONE MORE POWERFUL BENEFIT

In addition to the many benefits we've mentioned over the past eight weeks, there is yet one more powerful benefit of knowing your purpose. It is the benefit of having God's "spoken blessing" poured into your life.

The most memorable story depicting the importance of a spoken blessing can be found in the book of Genesis. It is the story of two brothers, Jacob and Esau.

Jacob knew the irrevocable power of his father's spoken blessing, but he also knew—as the second-born son—he was not the rightful heir. As was the custom of the day, his father Isaac could choose to give his blessing to a more worthy son rather than his firstborn. But Jacob was not content to wait for God—or his earthly father—to make that decision. Jacob and his mother devised a plan to trick the aging father and get him to unknowingly grant the blessing to Jacob.

To get the whole story, check out Genesis 27. But for our purpose here, know that the father's blessing was powerful and it was irrevocable once given. Jacob would have gone to any length to get that kind of blessing. Although Jacob's trickery would cost him dearly, the power of his father's blessing was on his life from that point forward.

How does this apply here? We are convinced that the power of a spoken blessing can have lasting power and benefits. To have your mother or father—

or someone else you admire and respect—tell you they see amazing potential in you—can unleash possibility that would otherwise never come forth. For your earthly father to say you are loved, that you are great in his eyes, and he knows you can do amazing things—we believe that releases a blessing of confidence and strength like nothing else he could ever say to you.

power of a spoken blessing

Sadly, many of us have never had anyone speak this kind of blessing over us. Our earthly fathers and mothers may not be willing or able—they may not even be alive to do so. But there is another option. What about being able to get this kind of blessing from your heavenly Father?

When you seek the Lord and receive your identity and destiny statements, we believe you are receiving a powerful blessing directly from God the Father who planned, created, and gave you life. When God says, "This is who you are in my eyes, and here's what you were created to do," it releases a blessing that is powerful and life-altering!

Take time now to write a brief prayer below, and talk to God about what is on your heart when it comes to blessings. For some it will be a prayer of thanks. For some it may be chance to really embrace your purpose statements and receive the blessing you never received here on earth.

DIVE DEEPER

To learn more about the power and importance of blessings, we recommend *The Power of the Spoken Blessing* by Bill Gothard, who says,

"God bless you!" is for most people nothing more than a vague cliché. But to those who realize its full meaning and potential, it is a powerful spiritual weapon that is capable of marvelous results."

Find this book at http://billgothard.com/bill/teaching/spokenblessings/

NEXT STEPS

Through the **7 Steps to Purpose** you have learned what it means to listen for the Lord, and then navigate life one step at a time based on His direction. To help maintain that approach, we want to lay out your next steps.

Without a plan of action for living the purpose God has revealed, there is little likelihood that it will actually happen. As the old saying goes, "Everyone ends up somewhere, but few people end up somewhere on purpose." We would add, few people end up somewhere on purpose unless they have a plan and are willing to diligently work it!

So, let's look at a few things you can consider as you go forward.

GUIDELINES FOR GOING FORWARD

Use your purpose statements as decision-making lenses:

- List all of your activities and involvements on a sheet of paper.
- Evaluate each item through the lens of your identity and destiny.
- If the activity, relationship, or endeavor is not in alignment with your purpose, consider taking steps to eliminate it from your life.
- Use this same process to evaluate future activities and involvements. This is how you can experience a power that very few people possess—the power to say "no" because your "yes" is so big.
- Use "purposefulness" as a primary criterion when making decisions.
- Always, seek the Lord for His guidance and confirmation.

Set aside regular times to speak with the Lord:

- Use the spiritual disciplines you've learned through this program. Spend time listening and journaling with the Lord on a regular basis. The only person who loses by not doing this is you. The Lord wants to talk with you, and you now have tools that can help you keep the lines of communication open.
- When you have so much to gain, and so very little to lose—go for it.
- Use a "no-excuse" attitude about maintaining a daily quiet time with the Lord and using these disciplines.

Repeat your identity, destiny, and assignment statements out loud, no less than daily:

- Post your purpose statements in a place where you will see them regularly. Use sticky notes, index cards, or whatever it takes. This will keep purpose in the forefront of your mind, and make it a stronger force than other driving influences in your life.
- You need to own your purpose statements. They need to become the very foundation of your life.

Write a plan of action to make your purpose real and tangible in your life:

- Make a step-by-step plan of action, first listing the small things that can be done easily and quickly.
- List the larger, more-involved tasks, and break them down into their smaller elements or steps.
- Prioritize all your steps and tasks, and give a date for each to be implemented.
- Make your plan and work that plan.
- Make yourself accountable!
- Get outside help!
- If you do not work your plan and stay accountable, the long-term odds of achieving your purpose is not very likely.

live the purpose you've discovered

Change can be difficult and the tendency is to take the path of least resistance. Over the long haul, most people cannot "stay the course" and implement their plan of action without a little outside help and encouragement.
Finally, we don't want to scare you, but the forces of evil do mount up against those genuinely attempting to live their God-given purpose. The good news: The Lord is stronger than anything that can be thrown your way. Lean on Him and be diligent in prayer.

Getting the help of a trained coach, accountability partner, or outside "driver" to keep you moving toward you purpose may be the best thing you can do to ensure success.

YOUR FINAL ASSIGNMENT

As your **7 Steps** journey draws to a close, we often hear people say, "Don't leave me now. Help me figure out where to go from here. Help me determine how to live the purpose I have just discovered."

With those requests in mind, we have one final assignment: Go to our website (www.IdentityandDestiny.com) and get details on our highly effective follow-up program: **LIVE ON PURPOSE**.

LIVE ON PURPOSE is a step-by-step program guaranteed to exponentially increase your rate of progress and success as you pursue your God-given purpose.

your

story

is still

being

written

LIVE ON PURPOSE is a web-based program designed to guide you every step of the way. We help you assess your current situation, identify changes that need to be made, create your plan of action, and stay focused and accountable in the implementation of that plan. We help you continue to grow and strengthen your relationship with the Lord and encourage your ongoing use of the spiritual disciplines you have learned while introducing others as you progress in your daily walk with the Lord.

The greatest tragedy in life is not death, but a life lived without purpose!

Go to our website today. Get all the details about **LIVE ON PURPOSE**, and join this fast-growing community of **7 Steps** graduates who've not only been able to FIND and KNOW their purpose, but have now decided to LIVE it!

DESTINATION REACHED

Yes, we have now reached the destination we set out for when we started the **7 Steps to Purpose.** It is our deepest hope and desire that you have been able to crystallize your identity, destiny, and assignment statements as we wrap up our final day together. We hope to meet again in the **LIVE ON PURPOSE** program, but for now, we must say good bye and wish you all God's best as you pursue the hopes, dreams, and God-given purpose that have been laid before you.

We encourage you to keep seeking, listening, and working the spiritual disciplines of the **7 Steps to Purpose**. As you do, trust in the divine providence of God and His promises:

I know the plans I have for you…Plans to prosper you and not to harm you, Plans for hope and a future. Jeremiah 29:11

Trust that your life's story is still being written as you passionately pursue your God-given purpose. Stay in the will of God and above all, *do it well*. For one day, we look forward to joining you as we hear the Lord say, "Well done, good and faithful servant."

But for now, as our journey comes to an end, it feels like we are saying farewell to a dear friend. Know that you—and every person that God touches through the **7 Steps** program—have a special place in our hearts and we will continue to pray saying:

For this reason, since the day we heard about you, we have not stopped praying for you and asking God to fill you with the knowledge of His will through all spiritual wisdom and understanding. And we pray this in order that you may live a life worthy of the Lord and may please Him in every way: bearing fruit in every good work, growing in the knowledge of God, being strengthened with all power according to His glorious might so that you may have great endurance and patience, and joyfully give thanks to the Father, who has qualified you to share in the inheritance of the saints in the kingdom. Colossians 1:9-12

May God forever bless you as you live the purpose He has now revealed and so perfectly designed and created YOU to fulfill!

Scipture References

WELCOME

Jer. 29:11	I know the plans
John 10:10	that you may have life
1 Thess. 1:4	put his hand on you
James 1:5	ask God who gives generously

STEP 1: HOW ARE YOU WIRED?

Phil. 4:18	I am generously supplied
Rom. 12:4-5	members do not have the same function
John 10:14-15	I know my sheep
Gal. 5:22	fruit of the Spirit
Prov. 27:17	iron sharpens iron
Eccles. 4:12	a cord of three strands
Deut. 16:7	you must bring a gift
Heb. 7:7	lesser is blessed by the greater
1 Tim. 6:20	turn your ears to Wisdom
2 Cor. 4:8	struck down…not destroyed
Phil. 4:6-7	do not be anxious
Rom. 13:14	clothe yourself with Jesus
Matt. 26:41	spirit is willing
1 Thess. 5:16	be joyful always
Ps. 139:23	search me, O God
Zech. 7:9-10	show mercy and compassion
Heb. 12:1	run with perseverance
Ps. 34:4	he answered me
Rom. 12:2	let God transform you
Prov. 3:5-6	he will make your paths straight

STEP 2: WHAT MAKES YOU TICK?

James 1:7-8	double-minded and unstable
1 Cor. 13:13	but the greatest is love
Eccles. 3:1	a season for every activity
Ps. 119:105	a lamp to my feet
Rom. 12:2	do not conform…be transformed
Prov. 3:5-6	trust in the Lord
Rom. 12:4-6	we have different gifts
1 Pet. 4:10-11	use whatever gift
1 Cor. 12:1	about spiritual gifts…do not be ignorant
Matt. 7:7	ask, seek, knock

STEP 3: WHAT'S YOUR PASSION?

Jer. 29:11	I know the plans
Rom. 11:29	his call is irrevocable
Ps. 139:16	all the days ordained
Jer. 1:4-5	before you were born
2 Cor. 5:9-10	we must all appear
John 14:1	trust in God
Isa. 61:1-3	crown of beauty
Eph. 3:20-21	more than all we can ask or imagine
1 Cor. 3:8	each will be rewarded
Rev. 22:12	I will give to everyone according
John 21:15-23	do you truly love me

STEP 4: WHAT'S STOPPING YOU?

Ps. 139:13-14	you knit me together
Eph. 6:10-18	the full armor of God
Isa. 41:10	do not fear
Gal. 5:17	the sinful nature versus the Spirit
Isa. 55:2	eat what is good
Ps.18:29-30	with your help I can
Deut. 31:8	the Lord will go before you
Phil. 4:6-7	do not be anxious
Heb. 13:20-21	everything for doing his will
Isa. 59:1-2	iniquities have separated you
Ps. 139:23	test me…know my thoughts
1John 1:9	confess…God is faithful
John 5:16	confess to each other
Heb. 12:1	throw off everything that hinders
Gen. 1:26	create man
Gen. 1:31	it was very good
Ps. 121:7-8	the Lord will keep you
John 8:32	truth will set you free
Rom. 12:2	be transformed
Ps. 145:18	the Lord is near
John 14:27	peace I leave with you
Phil. 4:13	I can do everything through Christ

STEP 5: CAN YOU HEAR GOD SPEAKING?

Josh. 4:7	a memorial
James 4:8	come near to God
John 16:13	the Spirit of truth
John 10:3-4	calls his own sheep
Ps. 46:10	be still and know
Matt. 7:7	ask, seek, knock
Col. 4:2	devote yourselves to prayer

Jer. 29:13	seek me and find me
Ps. 1:2	he meditates day and night
Jer. 33:3	call to me
Heb. 4:12	word is living and active
Phil. 4:8	think about such things
Prov. 3:5-6	trust in the Lord
Dan. 2:19-22	mystery revealed…in a vision
Eph. 2:10	God's workmanship
1Pet. 5:6-7	humble yourselves

STEP 6: CAN YOU BE STILL AND LISTEN?

Jer. 33:3	things you do not know
Heb. 4:16	approach the throne
Ps. 111:10	fear of the Lord
Col. 1:9	wise with spiritual understanding
James 1:12	perseveres under trial
Matt. 7:3,5	speck of sawdust out of your eye
Rom. 12:17-18	do not repay evil
1John 1:9	he is faithful and just
John 14:26	Holy Spirit…teach you
1Cor. 2:14	only those who are spiritual
Jer. 29:1	I know the plans
Jer. 33:3	call and I will answer
John 15:5,8	I am the vine
James 1:6	believe and do not doubt
Deut. 8:3	does not live on bread alone
Prov. 19:21	plans in a man's heart
James 4:2	because you do not ask

THE ROAD TO SALVATION (LISTED IN CANONICAL ORDER):

John 3:1-8
John 14:6
Romans 3:10
Romans 3:23
Romans 5:8
Romans 6:23
Romans 10:9-10
Romans 10:13
Ephesians 2:8-9
Revelation 3:20

STEP 7: WHO AM I? AND WHY AM I HERE?

Matt. 7:7	ask, seek, knock
James 1:4-5	if anyone lacks wisdom
Exod. 3:10	I am sending you

Heb. 10:25	let us encourage one another
Gen. 27	story of a father's blessing
Jer. 29:11	plans for hope and a future
Col. 1:9-12	knowledge of his will

Tell a Friend—Start a Group

UNLEASH THE POWER OF PURPOSE IN THE LIVES OF OTHERS!

If you've completed the program, now is the time to share your experience.

- Recommend the **7 Steps** to friends and family
- Organize, lead, and help others assemble a small group

There's power in the group—power to support, encourage, bring insight, and share the excitement of discovering your God-given purpose!

GROUP LEADERS GUIDE

If leading a small group is new for you, consider Larry Kreider's book *What Every Small Group Leader Should Know*. It is a quick, easy read with lots of practical tips for how to organize and run a highly effective group study. It is on our recommended reading list at www.IdentityandDestiny.com and can be purchased from our site directly through Amazon.

Your role as group leader is not to teach. You don't need to coach or answer questions about the program. Your role is facilitator and servant leader. Your job (along with other "helpers" in your group) is to:

- Assemble the group and gain their commitment.
- Let them know where they can buy the workbook. (www.IdentityandDestiny.com)
- Build rapport within your group.
- Encourage relationship, openness, and confidentiality.
- Follow up to promote ongoing attendance and participation.
- Coordinate the meeting location and logistics.
- Keep your meetings flowing and honor the time established for ending your sessions.

Throughout the 8-week journey, your focus needs to be keeping everyone accountable, encouraged, open to learning, and praying for one another. If group members are having difficulty with program content or need additional help, please direct those individuals to us. We can be contacted through our website at www.IdentityandDestiny.com.

Launch your **7 Steps** group today—and have fun sharing the journey of purpose discovery.

Looking for Program Leaders

WE'RE LOOKING FOR PROGRAM LEADERS!

Attention:
Coaches, Counselors, Consultants, Therapists & Care Ministers

Becoming a Certified Identity and Destiny Program Leader could be just what you need! Now there is a way to explode the growth of your practice and deliver high-impact programs that produce life-altering results for your clients.

The Problem:
Finding enough time and resources to attract new clients, retain the ones you have—while developing and delivering high-impact programs that result in real, long-term life change—can be challenging, costly and time consuming.

The Solution:
Becoming a Certified Identity and Destiny Program Leader will provide everything you need to deliver proven programs focused on helping your clients FIND, KNOW and LIVE their God-given purpose. You will have access to the training and tools to lead small group conferences, deliver in-depth one-on-one purpose coaching, generate new clients through our website, and earn additional revenue as an affiliate. This all converts into enhanced financial returns and deeper fulfillment for you and your clients.

Benefits:

- step-by-step coaching and instruction
- exclusive access to all our proprietary materials
- ability to integrate our programs into your existing processes
- access to advanced coaching and training programs
- membership in our Private Program Leader's Forum
- access to all new programs and materials at introductory rates
- Identity and Destiny web-site coaching referrals
- invitation to our Annual Leader's Summit.
- access to our JV coaching partners—for top-level training and programs
- joint venture with I & D to promote your programs and products

And much, much more...Contact me now at *tom@IdentityandDestiny.com* to receive an application and details on this exciting opportunity.

You do the steps—God does the rest.